E REPROACH OF THE GOSPEL

THE REPROACH OF THE GOSPEL

AN INQUIRY INTO THE APPARENT FAILURE OF CHRISTIANITY AS A GENERAL RULE OF LIFE AND CONDUCT, WITH SPECIAL REFERENCE TO THE PRESENT TIME

BEING THE

BAMPTON LECTURES

FOR THE YEAR 1907

BY THE REV.

JAMES H. F. PEILE, M.A.

FELLOW AND PRAELECTOR OF UNIVERSITY COLLEGE, OXFORD
AND EXAMINING CHAPLAIN TO THE LORD BISHOP OF WORCESTER

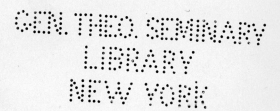
LONGMANS, GREEN, AND CO.

39 PATERNOSTER ROW, LONDON

NEW YORK, BOMBAY, AND CALCUTTA

1907

✠

TO MY FATHER

EXTRACT

FROM THE LAST WILL AND TESTAMENT

OF THE LATE

REV. JOHN BAMPTON

CANON OF SALISBURY

" . . . I give and bequeath my Lands and Estates to the Chancellor, Masters, and Scholars of the University of Oxford for ever, to have and to hold all and singular the said Lands or Estates upon trust, and to the intents and purposes hereinafter mentioned ; that is to say, I will and appoint that the Vice-Chancellor of the University of Oxford for the time being shall take and receive all the rents, issues, and profits thereof, and (after all taxes, reparations, and necessary deductions made) that he pay all the remainder to the endowment of eight Divinity Lecture Sermons, to be established for ever in the said University, and to be performed in the manner following :

" I direct and appoint, that, upon the first Tuesday in Easter Term, a Lecturer be yearly chosen by the Heads of Colleges only, and by no others, in the room adjoining to the Printing-House, between the hours of ten in the morning and two in the afternoon, to preach eight Divinity Lecture Sermons, the year following, at St. Mary's in Oxford, between the commencement of the last month in Lent Term, and the end of the third week in Act Term.

" Also I direct and appoint, that the eight Divinity Lecture Sermons shall be preached upon either of the following Subjects—to confirm and establish the Christian Faith, and to confute all heretics and schismatics—upon the divine authority of the holy Scriptures—upon the authority of the writings of the primitive Fathers, as to the faith and practice of the primitive Church—upon the Divinity of our Lord and Saviour Jesus Christ—upon the Divinity of the Holy Ghost—upon the Articles of the Christian Faith, as comprehended in the Apostles' and Nicene Creeds.

" Also I direct, that thirty copies of the eight Divinity Lecture Sermons shall be always printed, within two months after they are preached ; and one copy shall be given to the Chancellor of the University, and one copy to the Head of every College, and one copy to the Mayor of the city of Oxford, and one copy to be put into the Bodleian Library ; and the expense of printing them shall be paid out of the revenue of the Land or Estates given for establishing the Divinity Lecture Sermons ; and the Preacher shall not be paid, nor be entitled to the revenue, before they are printed.

" Also I direct and appoint, that no person shall be qualified to preach the Divinity Lecture Sermons, unless he hath taken the degree of Master of Arts at least, in one of the two Universities of Oxford or Cambridge ; and that the same person shall never preach the Divinity Lecture Sermons twice."

PREFACE

THE explicit directions of the Founder's Will relieve a Bampton Lecturer from the necessity of making the conventional apology for the publication of his sermons. Nevertheless, I admit that I am glad my book should go out to a wider audience than that which heard me patiently at St. Mary's. I hope that it will be read by many persons who are interested in religious questions. I hope that it will trouble their peace of mind ; and make them realize that the true " Crisis in the Church " is not ceremonial, nor, in any narrow sense, doctrinal ; and that it concerns all Christians as much as it concerns Anglicans.

I believe that the Church stands even now at the parting of the ways ; that, humanly speaking, the next few years will decide whether it is to shrink into a pietistic sect, or spread and develop, until it is actually the English people viewed in its relation to God. And I am not afraid to add that upon the Church of England, pre-eminently among religious bodies, lies the responsibility of making the great venture, or the great refusal. In making this claim, I think I am not inspired by any narrow spirit of party.   If I regard the Church of England as the appointed instrument of God for this end, it is not on account of its established position, its wealth, or its social influence; but because, with all its shortcomings, it has never lost the essential belief in the Church Catholic.   But the event alone can justify or condemn the Church; and the issue lies in the hands, not of the few, but of the many, the rank and file of Christians, lay and cleric.

It is perhaps not without significance, that, in the election of a Bampton Lecturer, the choice of the Heads of Houses should have fallen, for this year, on one who can claim no distinction as a Scholar, or a Philosopher, or a Theologian.   At any rate it emphasizes what I have tried to make a leading thought in my Lectures, that Religion is the immediate business, not of the expert only, but of the average human being.   At the same time my readers must bear in mind, that, wherever my argument obliges me to meddle with technical matters, I speak as a layman, and occasionally as a fool.   For instance, I am told that I have entirely mistaken the character of the Ritschlian philosophy: and I think it is very probable.   I maintain, however, that I have not misrepresented the teaching of certain nebulous religion- ists who prophesy in the name of Pragmatism.   Again, there are passages which my more advanced Socialist friends deplore as unpractical; and other passages, in which I am held to be unjust to non-Christian methods of reform and progress. Freely admitting my deficiencies, I am inclined to let the Lectures stand, for the most part, as they were delivered—if for no other reason, because my mistakes may be instructive, as illustrating the point of view of that common factor in human society, the ordinary educated man who is not a specialist.

Mere considerations of space forbid my mentioning by name more than a very few of those to whose written or spoken thoughts I have owed guidance and enlightenment.

When writing on the conditions of life and labour among the poor, I have supplemented my reading, and some little personal experience, by drawing unsparingly on the first-hand knowledge of friends who are actually working among the poor in London. I should like to make grateful mention of the Rev. H. St. J. Woollcombe, Head of the Oxford House; of Mr. A. H. Paterson, of the Oxford Medical Mission in Bermondsey; and of Mr. W. H. Beveridge, lately Vice-Principal of Toynbee Hall.

Those who are best acquainted with the work of Dr. Sanday will be best able to judge the extent of my indebtedness to him. But I have to acknowledge, not only the invaluable help which I have derived from his books, but also his extreme kindness in looking over the paragraphs in which I have dealt tentatively with the subject which he has made his own.

Finally, I desire to record my gratitude to the Rev. Charles Plummer, Fellow of Corpus Christi College, for his patient and sympathetic labours in correcting my proofs : a gratitude which is not at all diminished by the knowledge that he finds his chief pleasure in doing kind services for his friends.

LONDON,
   July, 1907.

SYNOPSIS OF CONTENTS

LECTURE I

THE FACTS

CONTENTS

LECTURE III

The Spiritual Need of Humanity

CONTENTS

LECTURE IV

WAR AND TRADE

LECTURE VII

CHRISTIANITY A REVOLUTIONARY FORCE

LECTURE VIII

SOME PRACTICAL CONSIDERATIONS

LECTURE I

THE FACTS

" As a matter of fact he who accepts either kind of Christianity must accept both; and, for my own part, if one could have one without the other, I believe it to be an easier feat to accept the dogma and refuse the ethics; indeed, a proof of it is that this is what the greater part of the world *really* does."—H. W. GARROD.

THE

REPROACH OF THE GOSPEL

LECTURE I

THE FACTS

"What could have been done more to my vineyard, that I have not done in it? Wherefore, when I looked that it should bring forth grapes, brought it forth wild grapes?"—Isa. v. 4.

1. In the subject which I have chosen for these Lectures —the question why the Kingdoms of this world have not long ago become the Kingdom of our God and of His Christ—the question why our Christianity does not make us better men and women—I am fully conscious that I am approaching a problem which may well overtask all that I have of courage, sympathy, and understanding. I may fairly be held guilty of presumption in putting forth in this place my thoughts on so wide and deep a mystery. In some things I shall have to say, I may seem to be judging wiser men than myself—in some I fear I shall offend better men—yet in conscience and honour I must go on. Constraint is laid upon me: because I am convinced that in the right answer to this question lies the key to all our religious difficulties, and I see that its importance is obscured

B 2

by a cloud of controversy on minor details of doctrine
and ceremonial.   Let me take, as an illustration of
what I mean, the Report of the Royal Commission on
Disorders in the Church of England, which was issued
last year.   It was a most grave and reasonable docu-
ment, worthy of its distinguished authors.   It was
eagerly awaited, and passionately criticized by men of
all parties.   Yet one must say that it contained no
word bearing on anything that can properly be called
Religion.   It dealt seriously and at length with mint,
and anise, and cummin ; and it dealt seriously with
them, because they are the things we care for.   I admit
that the real interest of the Report lies deeper than
anything that is explicitly discussed in it.   Doubtless
the real issue is whether the Church of England is to
go on in its present form ; an issue which must claim
the attention of every one of us, whether we desire or
fear to see that form changed.   But Christianity is
wider and older than the Church of England ; and if
experience really shows that it has failed as a general
rule of life and conduct, the question arises whether its
precepts can be allowed to stand any longer, even
professedly, as the guiding principle of humanity.

The paradox of sin existing and continuing in the
believer, as a metaphysical problem, exercises and
troubles the mind of the Christian Philosopher.   Nor
is it likely that a full and satisfactory solution will
soon be found.   How can we reconcile those two
passages so near together in the First Epistle of
St. John, "If we say that we have no sin, we deceive

ourselves," and " Whosoever is born of God doth not commit sin " ? [1]

I have not the learning or ability to propound any solution of my own; but I ask your patience while I try, with the greatest diffidence, to express thoughts which seem to me to cast light on the apparent contradiction.[2] I think we are justified by Scripture and Reason in believing that by the Incarnation the Son of God was made, not a man, but Man ; and that those who are being saved become, in a mystical but not in a figurative sense, members of the Christ ; and in the measure of their identity with Him are—not immediately freed—but enabled to free themselves from the power of Sin. The process of Salvation is gradual, and, as St. Paul testifies, is hindered by the impulses of the lower nature struggling against the sanctified will. Christ, for His part, has made Himself one with Man, by virtue of absolute love and understanding ; but He is not perfected until men, who are His members, by full self-surrender are wholly made one with Him.

The more obvious difficulties of this position are, I think, removed when we consider that succession in Time is a condition of human thought, and has no existence for the Eternal. *Sub specie temporis* the Sacrifice was accomplished once for all in Palestine nineteen hundred years ago. *To God* the Life and Death are part of the Everlasting Now.

[1] 1 John i. 8 ; iii. 9.
[2] See Dr. Armitage Robinson's edition of the Epistle to the Ephesians, esp. pp. 42 foll.

Thus in some degree we can apprehend that it is possible for us to fill up what is lacking in the sufferings of the Christ; and, alas, to contribute our share to the burden of sin which He bears upon the Cross.

I fully recognize that this attempt at an explanation must be open to criticism on many sides: at all events it cannot be in any sense complete or final; but it seems to me, as far as it goes, to be a helpful comment on a puzzling fact of human nature.

However, if the metaphysical problem were all, the average untheoretical man might safely relegate it to the study of the expert Theologian, and pass on his way. Unhappily it has an acutely practical bearing; and it is this practical aspect which I propose to treat in these Lectures. I shall inquire first whether Christianity has failed as we suppose, and then, what is the effect of this apparent failure on the actual everyday thought and action of the masses of the human race, for whom, as we believe, Christ died. And the inquiry, though it includes the occasional and repeated lapses of the devout believer, will look chiefly at the much wider field of the deliberate and systematic disregard of Christ's moral teaching by professed Christians, and especially by those who are not conscious of insincerity, or would be very reluctant to admit, even to themselves, that they are insincere or inconsistent.

2. It cannot, I think, be questioned that the striking contrast between the lives of Christians and the rules which they profess to accept is the great religious difficulty of the present day.

We are told that whole classes of our fellow country-men have drifted away from any kind of systematic religion, and that the chief cause of this departure is the impression that outward religious observances and the acceptance of Creeds make no difference in action and character ; that people who go to church are no better than those who do not.

The workman observes that the Christian employer, who in his private life is prominent in religious and even philanthropic activities, is to him just as hard and exacting a taskmaster as the man who professes no belief ; and he is being taught also to observe that the Church has for many years opposed every reform which has benefited the mass of the population ; and looked coldly on efforts outside legislation to improve the condition of the labouring class, such as the Temperance movement ; neglecting and thwarting them in their earlier stages, and only patronizing and exploiting them when they have established themselves without its aid.

We know that this charge against Church and Churchmen is not wholly true, but it is true enough to be widely accepted, and very difficult to disprove ; and the belief in its truth has incalculable influence in driving men, not only from the Church, but from Christianity.

I need not speak here of the poor man's objection to the Churches as upper-class or middle-class societies, in which he has no place and finds no welcome, because, as I shall show, this point is not at present relevant to

my purpose.   We may, as Christians, reasonably thank
God that we have been reawakened to the political,
social, and religious importance of what we call the
working classes, those who labour chiefly with their
hands.   Not only because they constitute a great
majority of the nation, but also for the sake of Him
who was called the Carpenter's Son of Nazareth, we
do well to regard the failure of Christianity to reach
and hold the working classes as a reproach to Religion,
and a calamity to mankind.

But it is important to remember that it is not on the
working classes only that creed and worship are losing
their hold.   With more educated men, doubtless, intellectual difficulties and an impatience of what they
consider antiquated ceremonial, have weight.   But they,
too, find a chief stumbling-block in the practical side,
the apparent ineffectiveness of orthodox belief to inspire
or control, and the impossibility of making their own
lives square with what they read in the Gospel, if they
are to hold their own in the struggle of professional or
business life.   Many, unable to give up success which
can only be won by unchristian methods, have the
honesty to relinquish the outward forms of a Creed
which can have no expression in their actions ; others,
less scrupulous, still go to church from custom or
because it is respectable, but more or less consciously
divorce the Sunday from the week ; too willingly convinced that maxims of conduct so commonly slighted
in the world, as they know it, cannot be applicable to
the affairs of daily life ; and, dearest loss of all, some

of the best spirits, *animae naturaliter Christianae*, are tempted to withdraw from a belief and a fellowship which make such high claims as directors of human life, and seem to them to effect so little.

3. At this point it is perhaps necessary for me to state clearly that I do not for a moment underrate or wish to disparage the effect which Christianity has had in the past and still has upon Society, and in a still greater degree upon individuals.

It would indeed be idle and ungracious to deny what Gibbon himself admits—the marvellous virtue of Christianity to revive and awaken the human spirit crushed under the weight of the dying civilization of Imperial Rome. The old order was doomed. It was the Church's office to console and strengthen obscure sufferers in the change ; and to tame and humanize the conquerors. Once more in the world's history the captive took the rough victor prisoner, not this time by superiority in art and literature only, but by the irresistible force of a higher religious belief.

A picturesque instance of this humanizing power of Christianity in our own country, and of the difference between the heathen invader, and the same invader still alien but now Christian, is noted by Professor Freeman in his essay on Glastonbury, British and English : [1]

" We read," he says, " in the Chronicle thirteen years before that fight at the Pens which made Avalon English—' Her Cenwealh waes gefullod.' Here then the Teutonic conqueror was one who had been himself

[1] " English Towns and Districts," p. 83.

washed, enlightened, made whole: in other words
baptized into the faith of Christ. Those whom he
conquered were his brethren. He came not therefore,
as Hengist and Aelle, simply to destroy. In other parts
of the West Saxon realm the coming of Cerdic and
Ceawlin had been as fearful as the coming of Hengist
and Aelle. But Avalon and the coasts thereof, the land
of the Sumorsaetan from the Axe westward, was the
prize of a conqueror who was Hengist and Aethelberht in
one. Under him the bounds of English conquest were
still enlarged; but English conquest no longer meant
death or slavery to the conquered; it no longer meant
the plunder and overthrow of the temples of the
Christian faith. The victor of Bradford and the Pens
had, before he marched forth to victory, done over
again what men fondly deemed to be the work of
Lucius; he had timbered the old church at Winchester.
He was therefore ready to spare, to protect, to enrich,
to cherish as the choicest trophy of his conquest the
church which he found already timbered to his hand in
Ynysvitrin."

I believe that the Christian Church was the nursing
mother of Western civilization. And Christian principle
has been, to within the last few centuries, the determining
factor of all social progress in Europe, even where the
clergy were not the ostensible leaders of the movement.
The Mediaeval Church was undoubtedly the most
democratic institution the world has ever known, and
gave such opportunities of power and dignity to low-
born talent as our modern democracies can hardly

parallel. I need not speak in this place of the Church
as the guardian of Learning; but it was the guardian,
too, of the gentler virtues, the virtues specially Christian.
It hallowed and exalted renunciation and self-control in
days when greed and passion were more unveiled, if
they were not stronger, than they are to-day. The
Christian element in chivalry gave it all that made it
respectable.

And even in later ages, apart from the great work
which has admittedly been done by the Churches, every
sound step in human improvement has been the direct
outcome of Christian principles. The Name of Jesus
might not be upon the banners of the advancing host,
sometimes, their leaders would have rejected it; but if
He had not been, they could never have fought and
conquered, for it was He who first effectually taught
men that the weak and the poor are precious in God's
sight, and that the strong are made strong to serve
them.

And while we acknowledge all that Christianity has
done for the world, we need not go beyond our own
experience to see what it can do for individuals; we
need not go to the great saints and martyrs to find
what we may prove by God's mercy in our own souls;
what certainly is about us in this prosaic modern world,
lives changed, ennobled, strengthened, sanctified by the
Grace of God. There is no cause but this which will
account for the mystery of the weak character—and all
are weak—passing unscathed through the fire of temptation; and the still greater mystery, when one who has

yielded to sin, and so diminished the power of resistance, yet finds strength to take up the burden of a
ruined life, and turns to climb the stony path of
repentance and amendment.   When we look thus upon
the holy and humble men of heart, and see their
courage, patience, and self-devotion ; when we see the
sinner's life amended, and his very character renewed,
we are stablished in the belief that a Name *is* given
among men whereby they may be saved ; our hearts
are uplifted to praise Him who grants such tokens of
His quickening power, a sign to them that believe and
to them that believe not.   "Then shall they say among
the heathen, the Lord hath done great things for them.
Yea, the Lord hath done great things for us already,
whereof we rejoice." [1]

And then, in face of other and commoner ex-
periences of life, the mood of exaltation passes, giving
place to a melancholy wonder why the Power which
can do so much, does so little.   We marvel at ourselves,
remembering how we have felt the love of Christ constraining us ; and have known the faith which is light
and power; and looked on sin for a moment as alien
and hateful ; and within the week, within the day, we
have coldly reasoned ourselves back to the calculus of
self-interest ; or, with open eyes and easy heart, cheerfully acquiesced in the promptings of desire.   And
more than by any act of sin we are appalled at the
dull, stagnant level of life in which we are content to
wander, incapable of aspiring to any height either of

[1] Ps. cxxvi. 3, 4.

righteousness or of evil. We know that others have not
failed as we fail ; that in every age the Spirit of God
has had His perfect work in some elect souls ; such
work indeed as only makes it more inexplicable that
their lives have not exacted the imitation, as they have
commanded the love and reverence of mankind.

Again, if the harvest is scanty and partial, yet
surely the seed was good. The teaching of Christ
stands for us the crown and flower of human morality :
not a system outworn and left behind by the advance
of the Race. To us the Rule of His Words and
the Pattern of His Life are an ideal, most nearly
approached by the noblest and best of men, the goal
to which we believe mankind are still advancing
by slow and devious paths, when they might attain it
directly, if they could receive His teaching freely and
unreservedly.

And if the seed be good, what shall we say of the
Sower ? When we consider to what origin we Christians ascribe our religion, what answer can we give
when we are questioned on the history of its dealings
with mankind ? "God so loved the world that He
gave His only begotten Son that whosoever believeth
on Him should not perish, but have everlasting Life." [1]
And man has contrived so to mishandle and misconstrue
Belief that the Faith of the Cross is to-day accounted
by thousands, in lands that have been Christian, a
thing foolish or mischievous ; by myriads more it is
quite removed from any control in the serious interests

[1] John iii. 16.

of life, and even to its professed champions it stands too often, not for the symbol and warrant of right conduct, but for the intellectual assent to propositions which are at best attempts to define the infinite.

When we look frankly at the present state of Christianity from these three points—its alleged origin, its actual merits as a rule of life, and its effect upon individuals, we are forced to confess that its influence on mankind at large is, and has been, strangely disproportionate alike to its high claims, and to the reasonable expectation of those who saw its beginnings; and if we take more than a merely historical interest in that disproportion, if we still believe that here and not elsewhere lies the hope of the world, we cannot sit content; we are forced to seek, as far as we may, causes and remedies.

4. It appears natural and convenient for the purposes of this inquiry to divide the history of Christianity into two periods: a long period in which no one seriously denied the historical truth of Christianity and its supreme ethical value, and a shorter period, bringing us down to the present day, in which it is criticized, timidly at first, loudly and confidently later, as being ethically inadequate or pernicious. The first period seems to last from the time when the conversion of Europe was accomplished, at least to the middle of the sixteenth century. Isolated instances of revolt can be found early and at all times. But open blasphemers, like our King William Rufus, were commonly men of such frantic wickedness that they served rather to point a

moral than to shake the faith of others. The first
stirrings of a more refined and thoughtful scepticism
were confined to the speculations of a few scholars,
and made little impression on the public mind. And
if here and there a Ralph Tremur was too outspoken,
he could still be schooled and chastened by the fatherly
discipline of a Grandison; and the general feeling be
on the side of the bishop against the rash inquirer
into matters too high for him.

Age after age the nations of Europe rested in a
profound and unshaken belief that the historical and
doctrinal tenets of the Church were true and necessary
to salvation, and the belief carried its logical corollary
that those who denied or doubted those tenets were
enemies of the human race. The strength of this
conviction is shown by the history of the word
"miscreant"—the man who believes amiss is counted
capable of any crime; it is shown in the attitude of
Christian Europe towards Mohammedans, and by the
popular feeling against the Jews, which found its
expression in the stories of William of Norwich and
little Saint Hugh of Lincoln; stories which have their
exact parallels in Eastern Europe to-day. The massacre
of the Albigenses, with every circumstance of cruelty
and perfidy, was accepted by Civilization as an act of
righteous and salutary retribution. The powerful
Order of Templars fell unpitied under a charge of
celebrating profane rites. The severest treatment of
heretics was regarded as just and necessary; and the
heretics suffered and died, not for opposing Christianity,

but for clinging obstinately to their own conception of it.

And this unquestioning faith did not confine itself to the dogmatic side of the Church's teaching, in spite of the perpetual and often dominant tendency to set orthodoxy above morality. The primary importance of right doing, though obscured by mechanical methods of salvation, was faithfully preached by the clergy, and was accepted by the sound instinct of the people. When a greater Hugh of Lincoln pointed to the Last Judgment in the Church at Fontevrault, and bade trembling John mark the end of princes who do that which is evil in the sight of the Lord, neither king nor bishop was troubled by questionings as to the sufficiency of the Gospel Rule to meet all cases. The pattern of the Perfect Life given by Christ was acknowledged by all men as absolute, however far their practice might vary from the received standard.

We are naturally inclined to date the beginning of the second period from the Reformation; and it is certainly true that the religious break-up of the sixteenth and seventeenth centuries gave an impulse to the intellectual movement which ends in scepticism. But we must acquit the Reformers of any intention of freeing thought in religious matters. Their purpose was wholly to ascertain and enforce the essential truths of Christianity; and by their readiness to persecute they gave a melancholy proof of the sincerity of their convictions.

In fact it is difficult to assign a definite date at

in fratricidal strife, betrayed to death by the trappings
they have borrowed from the world and the devil :

> telis
> Nostrorum obruimur : oriturque miserrima caedes
> Armorum facie, et Graiarum errore iubarum.[1]

And because they have no flag, no watchword, no credo,
to unite them and to inspire them, the strong man
armed still keepeth his palace. But the step of One
stronger than he is even now at the door. Who shall
that stronger be ? Must we not ask, as the Baptist
asked of old, with heart searchings, that mistrust not
Him but ourselves, " Art Thou He that cometh, or look
we for another ? "

5. What is to be the spiritual force which shall teach
men the meaning of life, and evolve harmony and order
from the mental and moral chaos in which mankind are
struggling ?

There are some earnest people who would have us
believe that the Gospel of Jesus of Nazareth has indeed
been a message of salvation in the past ; but now its
day is done, its power passed away for ever. They look
for the dawn of a new Religion which shall replace it,
as it replaced the outworn creeds of the ancient world.
They cry to us, " Lo, here is the Christ, or lo, there ; "
but we believe them not. We cannot tell what the
future may bring forth ; but certainly we do not find in
anything they offer us so far, the note of an authentic
revelation, nor in their methods any hope of it. We are

[1] Virgil, Aeneid, II., 410.

sure, at least, that a World-faith can never spring from the travailing of self-conscious intellect. And meanwhile, till the new Gospel shall have approved itself, we cling, not unreasonably, to the old. It may be that we have toiled all the night and taken nothing ; but in the dawn we look for, we trust that we shall yet see our Risen Lord upon the shore, and at His Word let down our nets for a draught.

Next, within the Church itself men of leading and authority urge that the best hope for the future lies in the restatement of the Creeds in terms of modern thought, that so the Christian Verities may regain their appeal to the conscience through the understanding. If this means that our conception of God must develop with the mental and moral growth of each succeeding generation, the process is not only desirable, but inevitable. But if it means an official recasting of dogma in the language of the twentieth century, then such a scheme might be summarily dismissed as impossible. It would not be easy, with the utmost freedom of choice, to select a body of men who would be at once qualified and willing to handle so thorny a business ; and one may fear that the deliberations of this ideal synod would be assisted by a multitude of counsellors in whom was not wisdom, and that all would end in a cloud of new controversy, and confusion worse confounded.

It may be true, though I think it is not, that the theology of the fourth century is so deeply involved in obsolete forms of thought and expression, that it has ceased to serve any useful purpose; but surely recent experience shows that it passes the wisdom of man to devise, in these days, a symbol which would command the assent of any one but its begetters. And even if it were possible—granted that a new Council could promulgate a new Creed received with general satisfaction—it is scarcely to be desired. The form the living truth takes to-day is still the paradox or platitude of to-morrow; and we should be in grave danger of consecrating new formulas to bind and offend the conscience of a not remote posterity. The weakness of our present position does not lie in the inadequacy of our definitions, but in the deadly fallacy of putting definition first and character second, for it is written, "If any man will do His Will, he shall know of the doctrine whether it be of God."[1] The road to Truth of Doctrine, which is the only guarantee for lasting unity of Doctrine, lies through reform of conduct—a journey infinitely slow, and in its early stages bitterly distasteful. It has not the picturesque attraction of great schemes for Corporate Reunion, but they are dreams—it is a reality. Now it is a hard saying, but a wholesome one, that the great majority of mankind have for centuries done everything with the Moral Rule of the Gospel except obey it. They have read it aloud in their churches and their homes; they have enshrined it in a magnificent system of worship; they have glossed and commented it, till it bears a suspicious resemblance to the code which they find most profitable

[1] John vii. 17.

and convenient; they have shaped and trimmed it to fit into a corner of an otherwise pagan existence.

But we must try once more to receive it in its entirety and simplicity; we must clear our minds of the conventions which dispense us from its obligations, and the exegesis which dilutes its meaning. We must go behind the mediaeval Church, behind the First Six Centuries, the Saints, the Fathers, even behind Saint Paul, and seek our inspiration once more where he sought it, in the Master Himself. I believe the secret lies in absolute unqualified obedience to Christ's plain teaching as He spoke it. That teaching, as we find it in the Gospels, is a small body of positive precept; it seems to me perfectly clear in meaning, and almost wholly ethical, laying stress on character and on conduct as the necessary test of character. "Except ye be converted, and become as little children, ye shall in no wise enter into the Kingdom of Heaven. By their fruits ye shall know them: do men gather grapes of thorns, or figs of thistles?"[1] To many of us so simple and difficult a Rule seems too little to satisfy the religious instinct. To others it seems too much for human weakness—a counsel of perfection. Writers, whose first interest is the moral improvement of the Race, declare that the morality of Jesus was meant for a little Jewish sect withdrawn from the world; it was never intended, and is not fitted to guide men in great affairs and complicated societies. And they have reason, but not so much as they think they have.

[1] Matt. xviii. 3; vii. 16.

It is quite true that His teaching is strangely at variance with the accepted standards and ways of life which we find in modern civilizations, and indeed in any civilization since the world first officially patronized Christianity in the reign of Constantine. But it is not on that account to be dismissed as impracticable. Rather, when we consider the pass to which the said ways and standards have brought us, this very antagonism commends it, inspiring a hope that an uncompromising application of it might produce results widely divergent from those which we deplore while we despair of mending them.

For me, then, and for those who have been my teachers, the hope of Salvation is not to be found in the possibilities of a new Religion which shall one day rise on the ruins of Christianity; nor, be it spoken with all respect, can it depend chiefly on the methods of a more enlightened Theology; though men who are seekers after Truth can never rate too highly the debt they owe to brave and patient workers in the fields of History and Philosophic speculation. For us the one thing needful is for mankind to recover the Rule of Life as Christ taught it, and to follow it, at whatever sacrifice; for we are convinced that if the answer to our perplexities, the remedy of our sorrow and sinfulness, be not in Him, then there is no remedy, no answer. "Lord to whom shall we go? Thou hast the words of Eternal Life."

LECTURE II

THE HISTORIC BASIS OF CHRISTIAN BELIEF

" The furnace has certainly been heated seven times over, and yet this group of facts, the common matter of the Synoptic Gospels, remains substantially unscathed. Doubts may be raised, but they will never permanently hold their ground. We have then, I cannot but think, in the criticism of these men an irreducible minimum. And that minimum, I must needs think, is an Archimedean point; grant us so much, and we shall recover what ought to be recovered in time."—SANDAY.

LECTURE II

THE HISTORIC BASIS OF CHRISTIAN BELIEF

" Forasmuch as many have taken in hand to draw up a narrative concerning those matters which have been fulfilled among us, even as they delivered them unto us, which from the beginning were eye-witnesses and ministers of the Word: it seemed good to me also, having traced the course of all things accurately from the first, to write unto thee in order, most excellent Theophilus, that thou mightest know the certainty concerning the things wherein thou wast instructed."—LUKE i. 1–4.

1. THE preface to the Third Gospel is rightly valued by New Testament students as recording frankly the writer's own view of the method and purpose of his work. These verses clear the ground for relevant criticism, by enabling us to dismiss various theories of the genesis of the Synoptic Gospels.

It is not till we understand what the Evangelist meant to do, and how he set about doing it, that we can usefully begin to judge whether he has attained his object, and really given us the certainty he promised. It was the purpose of the writer to ascertain by inquiry and comparison what Jesus of Nazareth actually did and said when He was on earth ; it is the purpose of New Testament criticism to ascertain how far he succeeded by those methods in giving a trustworthy picture of the events, and more especially of the Person, whom he professes to describe ; and to disentangle the genuine event, the authentic discourse, from the accretions of myth, or the glosses of theological tendency.

In the last century theologians and scholars were chiefly concerned with discovering what residuum of undoubted truth the documents would yield under the severe tests of impartial criticism ; and all schools of thought were practically agreed that the great issue depended on maintaining or discrediting the historical accuracy of the received account.

But to-day we are obliged to consider a previous question before we estimate the results of their long conflict, or even admit its importance. Time brings in its revenges, and by a strange irony it seems as if textual criticism and historical research, in their bearing on the problem of Religion, were in some danger of being relegated to the same limbo of futilities to which their exponents have long consigned the patient labours of the Schoolmen. If it can be seriously maintained that the objective occurrence of the events of the Gospel History is not a necessary condition of Christian Belief or Christian Morality, it is the refinement of pedantry to be disputing over dates and sources. The common sense of our forefathers would no doubt have rejected such a proposition as a mischievous paradox ; but to us the idea once suggested is not so easily disposed of, " for it is not so easy," as one of our most learned divines tells us, " to show how an event, or a series of events, in the past can affect the truth of a religion.

Either these events, to which so momentous an importance is attributed, form part of the regular series of occurrences in time, or they do not. If they do, they are only particular manifestations of laws which are always in operation, and which vindicate themselves continually in human experience ; except to the historian, it is not of much importance whether this or that particular occurrence has been accurately transmitted or not. . . . If, on the other hand, an event is purely miraculous and outside the regular series of cause and effect, its importance is in the inverse ratio to its strangeness." [1]

Such a separation between historical fact and religious belief will appear at first sight to the ordinary mind both difficult and dangerous ; yet it has been adopted by writers of very different schools of thought as a solution of the difficulty which the results of Biblical criticism seem to involve. Every one is familiar now with the Abbé Loisy's brilliant attempt, by means of the doctrine of development, to combine an extreme critical treatment of documents with an *ex animo* acceptance of the whole cycle of Roman Catholic dogma ; and Dr. Inge, in the essay from which I have just quoted, makes it clear that the attitude towards the historical side of Christianity taken up by Loisy, and, in a way more intelligible to me, by Father Tyrrell, in his book, " Lex Orandi," and its sequel, " Lex Credendi," differs little from that of the liberal Protestant followers of Ritschl, who by their theory of Value Judgments make spiritual

[1] Dr. W. R. Inge, "Truth and Falsehood in Religion," p. 91.

need, and not harmony with objective fact, the criterion
of religious truth in a doctrine. Dr. Inge goes on to
criticize this attempt to escape from a difficult position
by lifting the whole subject above the verdict of history.
He points out that it fails on its own ground, being
psychologically inadequate to satisfy the religious
instincts of those who really believe the supernatural
occurrences alleged ; while for those who already accept
them merely as symbols, it is superfluous. The simple
believer, alarmed by the frank dealings of the critics
with what he has been taught to consider the Word of
God, is at first attracted by a line of argument which
seems to "put the Ark of God somewhere where the
Philistines cannot get at it;" but as soon as he under-
stands whither the seeming easy path is leading him,
he turns back startled and dismayed, and perhaps *not*
destined to find again the old guides he has deserted.

I think it is necessary to insist on this practical
danger ; for to propound views of Truth which are sure
to puzzle and offend simple minds, is to lay a stumbling-
block in the very gate of salvation.

A Gospel which depends upon fine distinctions is
no Gospel to preach. And it is no answer to say that
the same Truths may be presented in one form to the
uneducated, while they are held in another form by
the wise. Certainly religion can never be quite the
same thing to the learned and to the ignorant. But
the day of an esoteric doctrine, opposed on such a
vital point to popular conceptions, is past, if it ever
existed ; a lively interest and curiosity about religious

subjects is so widespread, if thinly spread, in our time, that Reserve has become impossible. And if it were possible, the fact remains that the preacher, to be effective, must believe sincerely in his message. We may no doubt rightly welcome the pragmatist doctrine as a scientific statement and explanation of certain phenomena of the religious consciousness. It is valuable as denouncing the fiction of pure reason apart from will and emotion, and rejecting its long-standing claim to be the sole guide of life and instrument of belief. It is very valuable in its insistence on right action as the proof of right belief, in its not unneeded reminder that, " All our postulates must stand the test of practical working before their claim to truth can be admitted. Whatever our faith, it must be confirmed by works, and so prove itself to be objectively valid." [1]

It is of course plain, from what I have said in my first Lecture, that practical teaching of this kind must have my full and unfeigned assent. But I venture to suggest that the pragmatist is false to his own canon, and is falling again under the dominion of pure reason, when he carries his principle to its extreme logical conclusion, and offers us the conduct-value of a belief, not as a note of historic truth, but as a substitute for objective fact. The centre and essence of Christianity lies in the Person of Jesus Christ, and I believe that to nine-tenths of the human race it would be idle to offer what the philosopher may call an ideal, but the

---

[1] F. C. S. Schiller, " Faith, Reason, and Religion."—*Hibbert Journal* for January, 1906.

plain man would call an imaginary Person. The writers whose views we have been discussing virtually attempt to show that if the Gospels should be proved a myth, it would make no difference to Christianity. I am not of their opinion. I trust that we should be able to face such a disaster with courage and sincerity. I do not suggest that the belief in God and Right would perish from among men; but I do maintain that it would be a stupendous check to the spiritual and moral progress of the human race: the loss of the most illuminating revelation of God, the most powerful motive that the world has ever known.

2. So far I have spoken of intellectual movements which are conservative in their apparent radicalism, having for their professed purpose an attempt to preserve the effective belief in Christ by fitting it to the conditions of modern thought. It is clear that whatever objections apply to purely subjective conceptions of Religion, will in our view apply still more strongly to ethical systems which ignore altogether the religious sanction, finding an adequate explanation of the moral sense in a natural evolution determined by natural motives of selfishness.

Many who accept this account of the genesis of morality regard the teaching of Christ as a real but quite normal step in the evolution of moral ideas, while others condemn it as retrograde, and as obscuring the real issues by the introduction of false motives and irrelevant sanctions. But to all alike it is but a movement or an eddy, like others, in the natural stream of progress. It is here that the Christian is in conflict with the secular moralists. First, he sees in the natural selfish impulse the ·bar to moral progress, and cannot admit that what he finds the chief hindrance to right conduct in his own life, and in the world about him, can also be the source and origin of the rules it contravenes. Second, the Christian is convinced that in Christ we have a real and unique moral revelation. I am not concerned to deny that much of the morality of the Gospels exists, or may be conceived to exist, independent of its historical setting : that much of it is actually to be found elsewhere. And by this I do not merely mean that many of our Lord's recorded sayings can be closely paralleled from the best Jewish Literature of a time before His Birth. I mean to admit frankly that a measure of His Spirit, which is not always discernible in His professed followers, may be found in Greek and Oriental Religions and Philosophies. Probably its most notable manifestations are in the precepts of the purer Buddhism, and the teaching and character of the Platonic Socrates. It is not surprising that Christian writers have credited Plato with direct divine inspiration, nor would it be easy to find a reasonable theory of inspiration on which we can call them wrong. It is not merely in the great passages which centre round the death of Socrates that we are constantly moved by resemblances of thought and even of word to the Gospel story; everywhere we find anticipations of ideas and principles which we have too easily accustomed ourselves to regard as exclusively

D

Christian. Without going beyond the limits of that portion of one book [1] with which my work in Oxford has made me more familiar, we have the picture of the non-aggressive state, in how many things the type in large of what we expect in the Christian man. We have the important distinction between the exercise of an art with a view to gain, and its exercise for its own sake, which in the light of Plato's conception of Virtue as the Art of Life, is a much-needed warning of the true basis of moral action. And, not to multiply instances, the whole character of the φύλακες, with their great powers and privileges to be used solely for the good of the whole Society and of the weaker and less wise brethren, is profoundly Christian, and recalls to us sharply what should be the character of disciples of One who came not to be ministered unto but to minister.

We shall not deny to Plato, nor to Sakya Mouni, a portion of the Divine Spirit. We believe, in a wider sense than the writer of the Epistle to the Hebrews, that God of old spake to our fathers πολυμερῶς καὶ πολυτρόπως, by divers portions, and in divers manners; but we believe also that He hath spoken to us in His Son. Great as has been the influence of Platonism on human thought, its influence on human life has not been great, nor always good. His mysticism carries him out of touch with the rough and ready dealings of human life, and was quickly superseded by the positive philosophy of Aristotle, with *its* ideal of the prosperous

[1] Plato, Republic, I.–IV.

pagan gentleman, so curiously resembling the type which we accept with satisfaction in a world which is again, or still, pagan.

But it may be urged that if Plato failed to commend a gospel of self-renunciation and self-discipline to a selfish generation, Buddha at least commended it, to a degree, and with a practical effect, which Christianity cannot rival. This is true; and yet I venture to maintain that when we have given all credit possible to non-Christian systems of ethic, it remains that Jesus Christ revealed two new things—a new character and a new religion. The character He revealed is new in this: that Christian unselfishness has a quality quite distinct from the Buddhist self-renunciation, which is, in a sense, purely selfish in its spirit and aims. The Buddhist wants to be rid of his individuality as an obstacle to the higher life, Nirvana; and for this end he is ready to sacrifice his fellow-men, in so far as he deprives them of his services and companionship. The Christian's Self is profoundly interesting and infinitely precious to him because he is a Member of Christ, a necessary atom in the completeness of the divine Cosmos, a note in the divine harmony—

> " His voice seems weak: it drops:
> Creation's chorus stops."

The perfected Christian cannot strictly be said to sacrifice his interests to others or to the community—that belongs to the period of conflict and imperfection—but he makes their interest his; he finds self-realization in identifying himself with his brethren, and sets on their personalities the same value and interest as on his own, for the same reason. And this spirit of universalism, which makes men truly brethren, makes them also Sons of God; it is the spirit of adoption whereby we cry, "Abba, Father."

This new character, founded on the conviction of the infinite value of each human soul to itself, to God, and to all other human souls, makes of Christianity a new Religion. All the other Religions the world has known are either exclusive or non-moral, and most of them have both defects. For the Israelite, Jehovah had indeed become in the course of ages, not only one God, but the One God, supreme and alone in the Universe; but His favour belonged only to those who were children of Abraham by blood or adoption. The life of the Gentile nations was shadowed by the presence of their Gods, and made up of religious observances; but their religion of daily life was non-moral; its moral aspect was reserved for the few—for persons of intellectual culture and leisure, or in some way separated from the kindly race of men. The Religion which Christ teaches has neither limitation; its scope not only may, but must, include all human beings either as subject or object. Its morality is not a "cloistered virtue." We read, as last and chiefest of the signs which were to confirm the troubled faith of the Baptist, that "the poor have the gospel preached unto them." Poverty in this place means surely, not only the lack of pence, but the lack of leisure, the supposed ignorance of higher things, which is the portion of all who are occupied in carrying on the world's work, whose lot is cast in the busy fields, and not in the quiet garden of the Lord.

3. Having thus expressed to the best of my power what I conceive to be the distinctive character of the Christian ethic, I propose to compare it with two systems which deal—the one empirically, the other after a more scientific method—with the alleged facts of human nature apart from God.

The first I will call the ethic of expediency, the real *Contrat Social*; the give and take which makes it possible for men to combine and live in societies, and is frankly based on self-interest. I will borrow from the "Republic" a description of its origin, which is also a criticism of its defects.

"To commit injustice is, they say, in its nature a good thing, and to suffer it an evil thing; but the evil of the latter exceeds the good of the former; and so, after the twofold experience of both doing and suffering injustice, those who cannot avoid the latter and compass the former find it expedient to make a compact of mutual abstinence from injustice. Hence arose legislation and contracts between man and man, and hence it became the custom to call that which the law enjoined just as well as lawful. Such, they tell us, is justice, and so it came into being; and it stands midway between that which is best, to commit injustice with impunity, and that which is worst, to suffer injustice without any power of retaliating. And being a mean between these two extremes, the principle of justice is regarded with satisfaction, not as a positive good, but because the inability to commit injustice has rendered it valuable; for they say that one who had it in his power to be unjust, and who deserved the name of a man, would never be so weak as to contract with any one that both the parties should abstain from injustice." [1]

This, we must admit, is not really an unfair statement of the principle on which a large proportion of men have always acted in government and business; and we may further admit that within strict limits it has been partially successful; it does enable men, though with infinite dissatisfaction and friction, to live together in societies. But it is obvious that for the real work of Ethic, the formation of character, it has little value; and that indirect, and based on a misconception of its true nature. Since its real sanction is simply a balance of advantage, it will break down wherever the advantage appears to be on the other side— that is, in every case of strong temptation. In a certain proportion of cases these revolts will be successful; and the rebel having first defied the law, will next proceed to remould it to the advantage of himself or his class, and to the detriment of those who are not strong enough to resist. Thus, as Thrasymachus brutally but quite truly maintains, the ethic of expediency works out as the interest of the stronger. The breaker of the old contract is in a position to dictate the new, and

[1] Plato, Republic, 358, 359, Davies' and Vaughan's translation.

assumes a virtue in observing the terms of injustice which he has formulated. " The kings of the Gentiles exercise lordship over them, and they that exercise authority are called benefactors."

But the position of the encroacher is still insecure, so long as it is protected by no stronger defences than he has broken through to attain it ; and therefore we see in the next stage, Power founded on no other claim than the strong hand, seeking to hedge itself about with transcendental sanctions, divine right of kings, and the like ; thus confessing that the ethic of expediency has in itself no obligation to bind the will and the conscience. But in fact it found little difficulty in imposing such sanctions. The human mind, with its innate reverence for law and custom, eagerly accepts the claim of an immemorial and sacred origin for institutions which date back beyond the memory of its own generation. When Shakespeare puts it into the mouth of the vile Claudius, the usurper of his murdered brother's throne, the words—

> " There's such divinity doth hedge a king
> That treason can but peep to what it would,"

he does not write only in tragic irony. His genius touches a deep-rooted instinct, which makes men pay a superstitious respect to power and success in the most unworthy.

The word " divinity " recalls to us the Zeus-born princes of the Iliad, but it has another and more sinister significance. It reminds us that the Church has long been too easily inclined to ally itself with the

powers that be, as such ; it has given to secular govern-
ments not only the obedience that was due to them in
their proper sphere, but sanction and support in doubtful
or more than doubtful acts ; it has allowed the spiritual
authority to be invoked for the maintenance of established abuses and the justification of class divisions.
In the past the Church has had its reward, such as it
was, for these unworthy capitulations with the Spirit of
the World ; and to-day Christianity is paying the
price of them, and stands half paralyzed in the face of
a great opportunity. Men are beginning to find the
existing social order intolerable, and seek something
better than the haphazard rules of conduct which have
allowed it to come into being. They are weary and
heavy laden, but they will not come to Christ to be
refreshed, because in His Name burdens grievous to
be borne have been laid upon their shoulders. They
declare that the Churches have made the word of God
of none effect for them by their tradition ; and it is
useless to meet this complaint with indifference or angry
denial. We cannot blind ourselves to the fact that
official Christianity, instead of taking its place as the
natural leader of the new Reformation, is in danger of
falling with the old Order which it has tried so hard
to prop, and we cannot blind ourselves to the cause.
Just so far as the Church has been a steward of
unrighteousness, it is called upon to give an account of
its stewardship, and is suffered to be no longer steward.
The real ethic of the Gospel is discredited by the
practical ethic of those who have prophesied in its

name ; and men who are earnest for righteousness
are repelled from it, and driven back upon an ethic of
selfishness, a selfishness wider and more enlightened,
the modern scientific ethic, for which its advocates
claim all that is best in Christianity, unburdened with
dogma and tradition. Whether such a claim can be
justified time and experience alone can prove ; but I
may at least point out what seem to me fatal defects
in such a system, regarded as a general rule of life
and conduct. First, it depends on purely intellectual
motive ; and omits, and even renounces, the emotional
appeal which alone can move the mass of men to give
up what is immediately pleasant, for the sake of a
remote and higher good. An ethic whose cogency
admittedly rests on a wide outlook, and something of
a scientific habit of mind, is not likely either to
attract or compel any large proportion of men and
women, as we know them. Yet on this weak and
untried sanction it founds the tremendous demand that
we shall barter some of the pleasure and profit of our
little span of life to secure improved material conditions
for the Race in a problematic future ; and this heroic
venture of faith is asked, not from the strong, unreasoning impulse of self-sacrifice, but from the calcula-
tions of self-interest, which, however enlightened, has
always proved hitherto a weakening and disintegrating
force.

4. Let us, however, return to examine in detail the
claim to retain all that is best in Christianity, without
dogma—a prospect so attractive to many who value the

ethical side of Christ's teaching, but are troubled by
intellectual difficulties, or offended by ecclesiastical
assumptions. The claim is, as I have said, so far
untested by experience; for it cannot well be doubted
that great part of the best morality of to-day is an
inheritance, acknowledged or unacknowledged, from
Christianity. But we may judge whether tendencies
of the New Morality already ascertainable give promise
of preserving all that we most value in the old. First,
we shall observe, if I am not wrong, that a certain
class of virtues which we have been accustomed to
consider characteristic, Humility, Meekness, Long-
suffering, are destined to disappear as not making for
efficiency. But another and more fundamental opposition is found in the fact that the aims and the methods
of the new teaching are primarily material. "Seek
ye first the Kingdom of God," our Lord says, "and
His righteousness, and all these things shall be added
unto you." The secular Gospel begins at the other end.
It begins with the material environment, and is much
concerned with economics and hygiene, both of them
sciences which claim the right to disregard and even
to eliminate the Individual in the interest of the Race.
Thus scientific evangelists are at once in conflict with
the fundamental doctrine of Christianity, the equal
and infinite value of every human soul. They are
themselves not unaware of the contradiction, and
actually criticize Christianity on this ground, accusing
its supporters of short-sighted and sentimental humani-
tarianism, opposed to the true interests of the Race,

as indeed it would be, if we exclude religious belief from our hypothesis.

Meanwhile the general conscience forbids in practice the realization of any new schemes for promoting human advance on these lines, though it supinely allows the application of the principle in forms to which it has grown too well accustomed to be shocked by them. And indeed a better safeguard is found as yet in the fact that science is still nobly false to the logic of its own position. Let me take a striking instance. The true purpose of medical science is the physical perfection of the Race, and the shortest way to that end is not the nursing but the speedy removal of the diseased individual. The logical conclusion is plain : the principle is rigid and merciless. But in practice I do not hesitate to say that the healing art is the one sound and undoubted manifestation of Christ's spirit on a large scale now extant in the world. But it is the triumph of character over consistency. If we dethrone Christ to deify Science, must we not look with trembling for the day when Consistency will claim her own ?

5. I have given perhaps too much time to arguments which are after all likely to win the assent only of those who are already inclined to be convinced ; and left myself too little for considering the question which lies at the root of the whole problem. If it be granted that belief in a historical Christ is a necessary condition of the highest morality for the mass of mankind, how far are we justified in assuming that it is true ? An

exhaustive survey of the Historic Basis of the Christian Faith would be as much beyond the limits of a lecture as it is certainly beyond my powers. But I am encouraged to offer some considerations by the thought that, while the data and methods of research belong to the expert, the ultimate tribunal on a question of such intensely practical bearing must be average educated opinion, for which I may consider myself in some measure qualified to speak.

We must distinguish, I think, a first period in which criticism, chiefly literary, was avowedly hostile, and was met by a like animus for defending all that appeared to be threatened, without considering enough whether it was essential or defensible. The results for a time seemed to be ruinous to the orthodox position. The critics professed to have brought down the Books which compose the New Testament to a date which robbed them of all credit as historical documents; and the apologists, by maintaining obstinately much that was in fact untenable, weakened the cause they were trying to serve. It is very important to observe that much of the popular opinion, in England at least, which interests itself in these matters, is still at this stage. It is hard for us in Oxford to realize how many people still believe that the question at issue is whether the New Testament is verbally inspired and infallible, or simply untrue. Meanwhile for scholars the period of purely literary criticism is at least provisionally closed. An impartial application of critical methods has resulted in a return from the extreme negative

position ; and the general verdict of those who have
a right to speak is that the Books of the New Testament are substantially what they profess to be : not
what intemperate advocates of either party would
represent them to be. We may justly say that the
net result of treating the Bible as any other book has
been a great gain for those who value and believe in
Christianity. But we must be careful neither to over-
estimate that gain, nor to mistake its character. It
furnishes no excuse for a return to the old *a priori*
apologetic. The main Synoptic Narrative, the Acts of
the Apostles, and, with some reservations, the Pauline
Epistles and St. John, are apparently secure ; a
positive result which might have seemed beyond hope
not many years ago ; but at the same time we are
made painfully conscious that two great Articles of
the Apostles' Creed are left at best open questions by
purely literary criticism. And, on the other hand, a
chief gain of a century of free study and discussion is
that we can never go back to the old way of looking
at the New Testament as a single book of uniform
value and authenticity. It *was* an unquestioned
Authority. It *is*, I venture to think, a higher thing,
a source of knowledge which must be questioned relent-
lessly, if we are to discover its treasures. The acceptance of the documents as authentic and sincere has
supplied the subject-matter for a sympathetic but
uncompromising historical criticism, which has helped
us to understand the origin of Christianity, by giving
a human and living interest to events and actors that

an exaggerated reverence tended to make abstract and impersonal; and so in turn it leads up to what Dr. Sanday [1] calls ultimate problems, to the great question of all, "What think ye of Christ?" It is not a question that can be answered offhand, or by a mere appeal to the results of literary and historical criticism. Lest we should be tempted to conclude at once that our answer is inevitable, it is wholesome and instructive to consider a very different view of the same data; and to ask ourselves why we are not content to stop where it stops.

The theology of the Germans has always been notable for sincerity and profound learning; but the exponents of its latest phase claim our most serious attention by tendencies which are both new and striking: first, they have abandoned the technicalities of the study and made a vigorous and effective appeal to popular thought; and second, they agree in finding, in that part of the Gospel narrative which they accept, something which cannot be judged by ordinary standards; and yet, while their treatment of our Lord is entirely reverent, they steadily set aside the question of His Divinity, not so much denying as ignoring it. They set before us an historical Jesus of Nazareth: unique in moral insight and purpose, unique also in the character which is revealed by His life and by His death: who believed that He was the Messiah, and believed also that He was the Son of God in a sense, and with a fulness, that the best of other men may not venture to claim.

[1] "Outlines of the Life of Christ," Appendix II.

Thus Professor Paul Wernle, in his admirable book "The Beginnings of Christianity," writes of Jesus in language of profound reverence and sincerity—

"There was in Him something entirely new, a surpassing greatness, a superhuman self-consciousness which sets itself above all authorities, declaring God's will and promises, imparting consolation, inspiring courage, delivering judgment with divine power, a new mediatorship between God and Man, that left all the former far behind it."[1]

And of the Apostles after the Ascension he writes—

"The apostles were animated by a lofty self-consciousness. They felt themselves to be the representatives of Jesus. They were continuing His work; as ambassadors for Christ they were ambassadors for God. The new office of mediation between God and Man was continued by the apostles.[2] Wherever they appeared they stood in God's stead."[3]

And again of St. Paul, in passages for which I would ask your most careful attention, he says—

"Now St. Paul does not know Him" (that is the human Jesus of the Gospels); "he only saw the Heavenly Jesus, and that for a moment. . . . But facts prove that St. Paul knew Jesus in spite of all, yes, knew Him better than all his predecessors. What he brought to the Greeks was no mere product of his imagination, but the real Jesus, with His promise, His

[1] "Beginnings of Christianity," English translation, p. 55.
[2] *Ibid.*, p. 119.　　　　　　　[3] *Ibid.*, p. 139.

claims, and His redemption.   When St. Paul writes :
' He that hath not the spirit of Christ is none of His,'
and ' He that is in Christ Jesus is a new creature,' he
is filled with a profound and genuine impression of the
person of Christ." [1]

And in another place—

" It is just the Jesus of History that St. Paul
grasped with a deep and clear insight, as the Redeemer
who leads us . . . to the Fatherhood of God, and to
moral freedom, and who, besides setting the high ideal
before us, inspires us at the same time with strength and
courage for its realization.   It is for the living and
loving Jesus that the apostle's high Christology prepares
a way into the world." [2]

It might well seem, as it seems to me, that for those
who have studied the development of the Pauline
Christology there is, from such premises as these, but
one conclusion—the Divinity of Christ.   But Dr.
Wernle, and much modern Theology with him, refuses
to take the step, to draw the inference.

So much is granted to us and no more.   But do we
need to ask more ?   And with so much granted, is it
possible for us, is it reasonable, to rest there ?   The
evidence for Christ's Divinity rests on spiritual experience : ultimately on your experience for you, on mine
for me ; but in the recorded experience of other men we
may find confirmation for what were otherwise merely
subjective and individual.   And for this confirmation

[1] " Beginnings of Christianity," p. 267.
[2] *Ibid.*, p. 239.

we go unhesitatingly to St. Paul, St. John, and the Book of the Acts of the Apostles, of which the accuracy in detail has been so strikingly shown by the researches of Professor Ramsay in Asia Minor. There we find this conviction, growing indeed in clearness and intensity, but essentially primitive, and forming the ground of Christian preaching from the day of Pentecost onwards ; and, what is more important, so changing the hearts of mankind as to make them literally new creatures. And this conviction possesses the minds of men who were removed only by a few years from the time when Jesus lived and worked as an artisan in a country village. Some of them had seen Him hanging on the Cross, and touched His dead Body. It was not easier, but much harder for them than for any succeeding generation to think of Him as God. The more we simplify and humanize the Picture we take from the Synoptists, the plainer and more amazing is the miracle of early Christian belief. However much we simplify and humanize it, there remains an element which cannot be brought under rules and standards which apply to all other cases. It is, then, surely not permissible to accept the Synoptic narrative, and refuse the evidence of the Acts, the Pauline Epistles, and the Fourth Gospel as to its meaning.

We have a right to say that our assurance of the Divinity of Christ is not founded upon isolated and perhaps disputed texts, but on the impression of Him which we find reflected in the minds and souls of the men of His own time. And further, we have a right to

E

ask our critics, and are bound to consider most seriously for ourselves, whether the admitted facts of the first stage of Christian History are not accounted for more agreeably to reason by this hypothesis than by any naturalistic one that has been offered.

LECTURE III

THE SPIRITUAL NEED OF HUMANITY

"Quia fecisti nos ad Te, et inquietum est cor nostrum donec requiescat in Te."—AUGUSTINE.

LECTURE III

THE SPIRITUAL NEED OF HUMANITY

" Come unto Me, all ye that labour and are heavy laden, and I will give you rest."—MATT. xi. 28.

1. IN my last lecture I endeavoured to state the reasons which justify us in believing the historical truth of the events which reveal to us the Character and Person of Jesus Christ; and I tried to show that if they are historical, they are also unique in history, and cannot be fully interpreted within the limitations which apply to other facts of human experience. But historical truth of events alone, their uniqueness alone, does not constitute a gospel. A gospel must also have the power of satisfying a want. It is the call of the Perfect to that which is imperfect, and suffers in the consciousness of its imperfection. We recognize this Law of man's nature, not only in that higher part of his being which we call the soul, but universally. The meaning and value of all exact knowledge, whether historical or scientific, lies in its bearing on life. The progress of natural science is determined by the enlargement of man's physical needs. This does not mean that the motive of all scientific research to-day is consciously

utilitarian. We speak rightly of the pursuit of knowledge for its own sake; the need to be satisfied has
come, in many instances, to be an intellectual need.
But still the vast system of ordered and linked sciences,
which has taken all nature to be its province, must trace
back its origin to the half-animal desire of primitive
man to be fed, and warm, and safe; and must acknowledge that it has grown *pari passu* with his needs, as
they grew in number and complexity. Even so seeming-
abstract a science as Astronomy has its spring in a
practical need—

> "The merchant bows unto the seaman's star,
> The ploughman from the sun his seasons takes."

It is not by strength, it is not so much even by intellect
at first, that man has risen supreme above the other
creatures of the earth; it is by the quality of an heroic
discontent that will not accept limitations. Material
desires unsatisfied have driven him to search out the
secrets of Nature, and by knowing and obeying her laws
to enter upon his full heritage as her favoured child.
Spiritual longing unsatisfied leads him to seek the
knowledge of God, if haply he may find rest for his
soul in the assurance that the efforts of his finite will
are no longer random or mischievous, but in conscious
harmony with the Eternal Will.

2. The need of Religion depends upon the fact of
Sin.[1] Now we most of us know very well what we mean

---

[1] It has been pointed out to me that these words, taken literally,
would imply that sinless beings have no need of Religion. That is
not my meaning. But I have let the sentence stand, because, for

by sin; but it is not easy to define in set terms, partly because it belongs to the spiritual sphere which has no terminology proper to it, so that we are in fact compelled to approximate to our meaning as best we can by metaphor; and partly because the idea of it has been confused by centuries of partisan theology, which has taken one or another metaphor for absolute truth in its speculation on the nature of Sin, its causes, and its remedies. Nevertheless, I believe that it is in the enlightened Christian doctrine of Sin that we shall find the most complete and scientific account of the phenomena, and learn what sin is, and what it is not.

It is a real thing, not an illusion. It is not purely negative, like the shadow a strong light casts; or like cold, which is merely the absence of heat. It is not a stage in the evolution of goodness, but an active principle making against goodness. Finally, it is not merely deficiency or failure, but something existing permanently in its effect on the soul of the sinner, and his relation to God. Different aspects of it are presented by the similes of a burden which galls and bows down its bearer; a ferment which taints and assimilates to itself the wholesome substance into which it has found its way; a disease which paralyzes the will to do right, as physical disease distorts and cripples the body.

So vivid and alarming a realization of sin as a positive factor in the complex of human affairs is apt to

fallen humanity, I think it is true. It is the fact that without God "the efforts of his finite will are random or mischievous," and the sense of this fact, which bring to man the need of Religion.

be meaningless or offensive to an age of material prosperity and scientific advance.   It is condemned as
producing a morbid habit of introspection, and, in
practice, as a hindrance to progress.   Science, in effect,
borrows the saying of St. Paul, and bids men forget the
things that are behind and reach forward to the things
that are before—

"As a matter of fact, the higher man of to-day is
not worrying about his sins at all; . . . his mission, if
he is good for anything, is to be up and doing." [1]

The phrases, torn from their context, have become
familiar, almost classical, though really their writer, as I
hope to show, before he has told all his mind, restores
to us more than he has seemed to take away.   However,
let us take the words, as he offers them, for the utterance
of Orthodox Science.

"The higher man of to-day is not worrying about
his sins at all; his mission is to be up and doing."

But surely the fact is, and the trouble is, that in all
vigorous activity for good he will find Sin, the sin of
other people, and more particularly his own sin, thwarting and hampering him at every turn.   This only needs
pointing out to be obvious, if the good work is social or
political; but even in the study and the laboratory men
cannot escape from the sins of sloth or self-indulgence,
and, above all, from the various subtle forms of deception
and self-deception whereof a cherished theory is often

[1] Sir Oliver Lodge, "Suggestions towards the Re-interpre-
tation of Christian Doctrine."—*Hibbert Journal*, April, 1904,
p. 466.

the fruitful parent. The higher man of to-day has need to be on his guard against all these, to say nothing of the oddly ecclesiastical sins of narrowness and intolerance.

But further, if the notion of sin at all is an offence to Orthodox Science, the notion of Original Sin is an abomination—or an absurdity. It declares roundly—

" As for Original Sin, or birth sin, or other notion of that kind, by which is partly meant the sin of his parents, that sits absolutely lightly on him. As a matter of fact, it is non-existent, and no one but a monk could have invented it. . . . An attempt to punish us for our animal origin and ancestry would be simply comic, if any one could be found who was willing to take it seriously." [1]

Well, I cannot help taking it seriously, because the spectacle of human beings suffering for the sins of their parents, and worse, being drawn almost irresistibly to sin by an inherited taint or weakness, is always before our eyes. I am quite well aware of the difficulty about the power and justice of God which follows ; but we cannot escape from a dilemma by ignoring the facts. And original sin, the natural tendency of the human heart to selfishness, appears to me to be among the least doubtable facts of our nature. It is there from earliest childhood, and, as bad men prove, and good men know, it endures while life endures. I do not cling to the theological term ; it is associated in some minds with extravagant doctrines and fantastic interpretations ;

[1] Sir Oliver Lodge, in the same article.

but in terms of Evolution, or any other terms, the thing is equally true ; the ape and the tiger are not dead in us ; and they will not die of themselves, but revive from time to time in most disconcerting fashion, if we do not worry about them.

I have suggested that the sense of sin tends to grow dulled in a time like ours, when the most powerful intellects are occupied with the exact methods and measurable achievements of Science, rather than with the unattainable ideals of Art and Poetry ; while the average mind seems to be chiefly busied over making money, and enjoying the apparatus of pleasure and comfort which money will buy. I will add, not that it proves anything, but for your consideration, that in the great creative age of the Christian era, the time when men did beautiful useless things for an idea, when they went on Crusades, and built Cathedrals, the sense of sin was vivid and dominant. Shall I remind you further that Robert Browning thought this one doctrine enough to justify a man in clinging to the faith which enunciated it ?

> " I, still to suppose it true, for my part,
>   See reasons and reasons ; this to begin :
>   'Tis the faith that launched point-blank her dart
>   At the head of a lie—taught Original Sin
>   The corruption of man's heart." [1]

3. Despite our impatient optimism, Sin is present with us, more dangerous in proportion as its presence is disregarded. When the symptoms of a disease are

[1] " Gold Hair : a Story of Pornic."

driven below the surface, its poison strikes inward, and invades the very seat of life itself. The sense of sin, unwelcome and discredited, revenges itself in the wide-spread and deep unhappiness of men and women who apparently have all the conditions of happiness. The phenomenon is accurately described in works on religious psychology, and must be familiar to doctors and to parish clergymen. Cases of it are probably not unknown to any one who is gifted with an ordinary amount of sympathy and insight. I am convinced, at any rate, that the thing is common—far more common, perhaps, than we are inclined to suppose. For such unhappiness, as a rule, is studiously concealed, and may easily escape the notice, not only of casual acquaintances, but even of friends and of near kindred. It may, and does, co-exist with a calm and cheerful demeanour before others, and with an active, healthy, fresh-air life, which gives no hint of the inward conflict. But behind the veil of self-control and normal everyday occupations the mind is deeply and miserably preoccupied with doubts and perplexities. It is filled with a sense of the horror and hopelessness of life; seeing the earth only as full of darkness and cruel habitations. And this *Weltschmerz* is, as it were, focussed in a more personal feeling: a deep, and, as it seems to the observer, unnecessary discouragement as to the individual character and conduct. Sometimes a very high degree of practical unselfishness is accompanied by an extreme sense of uselessness and failure. Such external activity for good without conscious enthusiasm, almost without interest, is remarkable;

and the account the actors in the tragedy give of it when questioned is no less remarkable. They explain their perseverance in right action and in the service of others as due, partly to the force of habit, and partly to the imperious need for escape from brooding thoughts; but stubbornly deny that it has any moral value, either objectively, or to their own character. They maintain that their acts are isolated and meaningless, not springing from any guiding principle within, and in turn not producing that feeling of comfort and power, which follows on really moral action. This is plainly not a complete account; but it is sincere and subjectively true. It is the want of a guiding principle which poisons the springs of happiness in action, and makes life dull and spiritless. Persons in this state are at once attracted and repelled by the traditional doctrines and usages of religion to which they are accustomed. The mind is very quick to catch at anything formal or unreal in worship, and to be disgusted by it. This hypercritical sensitiveness I attribute to an instinctive reverence for something which is felt to lie behind the forms, and to be dishonoured by shallowness and unreality. But in practice it makes people, and especially young people, cruelly severe and even unfair in their judgment of the professedly religious, and notably of clergymen, with whom they are brought much in contact; with the result that the sudden overmastering impulse to unburden their soul, which is characteristic, often carries them rather to a stranger, in whom they think they have detected the marks of a sincere and sympathetic mind. The first step in self-disclosure is naturally painful and difficult; but if it meets encouragement, the confidence which follows will be extraordinarily full and unreserved, proving the depth and poignancy of the need which cries for help. Complete frankness, however, does not by any means imply a spirit of complete docility to the chosen counsellor, or an unquestioning acceptance of advice and consolation. There is indeed a genuine and hopeful will to be convinced which has inspired the attempt. But, beside it, watchful self-distrust, born of long disappointment, is always ready to criticize new hopes and find them wanting. Any counsel which savours of mere authority or platitude is summarily rejected; so that if Religion be the remedy proposed, it must be, for the time, Religion in its simplest and least disputable forms—let us say Christ's own teaching, and a few of the more spiritual Psalms.

The condition of spiritual distress which I have described appears in some cases to follow on a definite emotional shock; for instance, the painful death of a near relative, or an enforced removal from a dearly loved home; or, again, on a sudden realization of the evil and misery of the world, such as might be caused by reading a book which exposes the intolerable condition of the very poor in our great cities. But in other cases these predisposing circumstances are absent, and even where they are present, it may be held that the crisis is determined rather than caused by the external stimulus. Again, a prolonged emotional strain, with its alternate fits of hectic activity and profound depression, is likely to react on the bodily health, and in turn to be reacted on by it. Yet the condition is not, in fact, pathological, to be treated with tonics and change of air, but spiritual. To put it plainly, what these people want is not a doctor, but a priest, or, if you prefer the term, a discreet and learned minister. I respect, and even share the British prejudice against the Confessional; but it is a grave question whether the Church of England has shown wisdom or courage, or indeed a proper sense of the value of her office, in dispensing with any organized system of spiritual direction; and I venture to say that many Nonconformist bodies make more account and more use of this Means of Grace than we do. Preaching may be all very well in its way, but it cannot touch, it does not even profess to touch, such cases as these, which demand a personal answer to a personal appeal, and cannot be reached at all by the most admirable generalities of the pulpit.

4. The answer which Christianity offers is the Incarnation. In the human life and Death of Christ, with its revelation of the Love and Fatherhood of God, and the Sonship of Man, it finds the guiding principle which lifts all life out of chaos into order; because in the realization of that Fatherhood and that Sonship, the ancient opposition of Self-love and Self-sacrifice is reconciled and lost. It is true that we were shapen in iniquity and conceived in sin, yet He came not to destroy the Law of our being, but to fulfil. When He

took upon Him to deliver man, He did not abhor anything that belongs to Man's nature. And therefore
His Perfection, tempted in all things like as we are, yet
without sin, is the hope of human life. For those who
look on it it is not the pattern only, but the motive
and the hope of attainment. If we are indeed one
with Him and with each other, if He is not made
perfect without us, then our dim strivings after good
are strangely transfigured; they have a significance, a
place in the divine purpose which they alone can fill:

"Ego dixi, Dii estis: et filii excelsi omnes,"

if we will; for Sin appears now less as the spirit which
denies ever, than as the spirit which refuses—refuses
suffering, refuses union with God and Man. The saving
wholesome sense of Sin is a sense of loneliness, of
separation from that Harmony to which our being
rightly belongs, in which alone the activity of our true
nature can find purpose and expression. In every age
it has taught men to seek God, if haply they might
feel after Him and find Him; but the Incarnation
alone can fully interpret and satisfy the restless yearn-
ings of the Soul. Let me put it in the words of the
eloquent spokesman and critic of modern Scientific
thought.

"The Sacrifice of Christ has convinced the . . .
world of Sin to an unique degree, of its reality and
dire consequence, of its unreasonableness, its aspect as
a disease that must be cured—with the knife if need
be, but cured: we have learnt that it is foreign to the

universe, it is not the Will of God, it is not due to His caprice, or amusement, or dictation, or predestination, or pagan example; it is something which gives even Him pain and suffering; it is something to be rid of, and there is no peace or joy to be had until unity of Will is secured and past rebellions are forgiven. . . . Forgiveness removes no penalty; it may even increase pain, though only that of a regenerative kind; it leaves material consequences unaltered, but it may achieve spiritual reform." [1]

This last sentence, with its unflinching insistence on a truth which we are all too ready to thrust from us, leads our minds to contemplate the mystery of pain and sorrow in the light of the Incarnation. Without that we are like men walking in the dark, guided vaguely by the voices of comrades in front, and earning a painful knowledge of the path and its direction from their own stumbles and wanderings, moving very slowly, yet moving forward. The experience of the Race, repeated in the experience of each life, has taught us something, often sorely against our wills, of the uses of Suffering. Our first animal instinct is to regard pain, physical and mental, as wholly evil, as the one real evil, to be avoided at any cost; we shrink from it in ourselves with horror, in others with disgust. I speak of this instinct as original and primitive, a thing which Civilization should long ago have put away; yet,

---

[1] Sir Oliver Lodge, *Hibbert Journal*, October, 1904, pp. 24, 25. See also in "The Substance of Faith allied with Science," Clause VIII., on The Meaning of Sin, pp. 52–55.

in fact, it is also a note of over-civilization, dominant in minds which value material comfort above all things. The belief that pain is the one real evil infects much of our social and philanthropic effort to-day, and is a chief obstacle to the acceptance of real Christianity. But short of Christianity, Reason and Experience teach us better things. Sooner or later we are forced to learn that suffering is the inevitable lot, not to be escaped by any of the sons of men. And after a moment of passionate revolt, we begin to understand that the inevitable is not, or not always, unnecessary and degrading, but in many ways beneficent. We acknowledge the broad justice of the punishment which Nature inflicts on the breaker of her laws; and are ready to welcome pain in its salutary office of warning us off from the dangerous places of life. It tells us of mischief—physical and moral—that may yet be cured, of the false step that need not be repeated. The burnt child dreads the fire, and is better, not for its burning, but for the bitterly won knowledge that fire is treacherous.

But the usefulness of pain does not end with the negative functions of punishment and prevention. As we grow older, we see for ourselves what we have often heard and only half believed—well for us if we see it *in* ourselves—that loss and suffering have a power which success and prosperity miss, a power to refine and strengthen the character; that the noblest work is done by sufferers, and through suffering; that pain is a condition of all true progress.

F

"The pleasures of each generation evaporate in air ; it is their pains that increase the spiritual momentum of the world." [1]

And last and greatest of all, we learn to feel, though we cannot tell why, that it is our common heritage of pain that unites us to our fellows, that comradeship in suffering draws men and women together closer than any other tie.   And when we have wholly learned that, we are not far from the Kingdom of God.   Pain is our Schoolmaster to bring us to Christ. What we have hitherto seen as in a glass darkly, the truth that we have learned bit by bit, puzzled and half unwilling, stands out suddenly with startling clearness and force when we see the Perfect Life compact of suffering.   The mystery is not logically solved, but it is set aside.   The path is still steep and rugged, but Day has dawned upon the travellers, and there is no longer need of the spoken word for guidance.   We forget the mystery of pain in the ministry of pain.

I do not wish to dwell much on the physical sufferings of our Lord ; doubtless they were all that the agonized body can endure ; but if we may reverently judge His manhood by what is best in our manhood, they were the least He had to bear ; and unfortunately they are connected in our minds with false and material views of the Atonement.   But the mental anguish, which is the portion of all true prophets, was His in more than full measure, heaped up and running over. It was not enough that His own nation rejected and

---

[1] Illingworth.

persecuted Him, His kindred despised and pitied; but all His life long His chosen disciples knew not what spirit they were of; they misunderstood and misinterpreted His teaching, and were disappointed in Him. Even after the Resurrection they ask, " Wilt Thou at this time restore the Kingdom to Israel ?" We judge them purblind and wilful; but what of us, of us, who, as they did, reverence His Person and acknowledge His Divine Mission ?

I fear most of us understand Him no more than they. The best we ask, the best we hope of Him, is that He will at this time restore the Kingdom to our little Israel, our beloved Church, our chosen Theory. The cruellest wrong of all still endures—

> " His sad face on the Cross sees only this
> After the passion of a thousand years." [1]

In pain, in sorrow, and in failure, He is made one with us; and suffering, His suffering and ours, has its perfect work in us ; not now as a dimly understood, half resisted Law of Nature, but as the Angel of the Passion, which brings us to His Feet, welcoming the sorrow which is the punishment and forgiveness of past rebellion; and when our souls are refined and tempered in the fire of affliction, raising us again to unimagined heights of love for God and man.

5. And now the question will reasonably be asked : If this is true, if some men have found enlightenment and salvation in Christ, why is it that the Incarnation

[1] Browning, " Fra Lippo Lippi."

does not enforce its claim on mankind as a whole, and in particular, why does it fail to satisfy so many of the earnest seeking souls who have felt the emptiness and confusion of life as they know it, and long above all things for a clue to the blind labyrinth? I ascribe its failure, where it does fail, chiefly to two causes—defects not in the Gospel, but in our way of presenting it, which I will call the Intellectual Fallacy and the Magical Fallacy. And by the Intellectual Fallacy I mean the mistake of making Theology equivalent to Religion, instead of regarding it as the study of Religion; much as if one should declare Biology to be identical with Life, and make it a condition of being so much as born that one should assent to a certain view of highly obscure and controversial questions in that science. I hope that this will not be thought an unfair or irreverent analogy, for it is certainly how the matter appears to many who would be ready to accept Christianity as the Key of Life, but find the way barred, as they suppose, by some dogma they cannot understand, some historical state-ment which appears to lack sufficient evidence. To have a right conception of God and of man's relation to Him is infinitely important; it is not very important to know, or agree with, what this man or that man has said about Him. It is only human nature to insist on that in which we differ from others: some aspect of doctrine peculiar to our sect, or grateful to our own minds. Still we are bound to remember that any doctrine, however sacred, loses saving power in so far as, and so long as, it is made the subject of controversy.

There *is* a test of fitness for admission to the Kingdom, but with our Shibboleths we are sometimes perilously near the position of those Pharisees of whom it was said, "Ye shut up the Kingdom of Heaven against men: for ye neither go in yourselves, neither suffer ye them that are entering to go in."

The Magical Fallacy is far older than Christianity, almost as old as the mind of man. Everywhere in primitive religion we come upon the belief that super-natural powers can be forced into the service of man by a knowledge and use of the right form of words, or of the right ceremonial.

The god is bound to grant the desires of the wor-shipper who knows the secret. Not faith but exact ritual can move mountains;

"Carmina vel caelo possunt deducere lunam." [1]

Hence followed the necessity of concealing the right method of approaching the gods, lest it should be copied and used against its proper owner, or neutralized by still more potent charms.

The religion of Israel, with its nobler estimate of the greatness and dignity of God, modifies the crude primitive belief. The obligation is now based upon a covenant or promise freely given. The effective formula is not imposed upon the Deity, but prescribed by Him; but in practice the result is the same. The old notion was too congenial to human weakness to be lightly let go, and in spite of the age-long protest of the prophets,

[1] Virgil, Eclogue, viii. 69.

a mechanical as opposed to a moral conception of religion held its own among the Jews ; it passed over into the Church, and strongly tinges all Mediaeval Christianity. A pleasing and innocent example of its survival is given in the Memoirs of a gentleman of piety and good sense who went crusading with St. Louis of France.

"There befell us at sea," he says, " a most wondrous thing.   We sighted a mountain perfectly round, which lies off Barbary.   It was about the hour of Vespers when we sighted it : and we sailed all night and thought to have made more than fifty leagues ; but next day we found ourselves off the very same mountain ; and the same thing befell us twice or thrice. . . . Then a worthy priest, called the Dean of Malrut, told us that they were never afflicted in his parish either with want of water, or with too much rain, or with any other affliction, but that as soon as he had made three processions three Saturdays running, God and His Mother delivered them from it.   This was a Saturday, and we made the first procession round the two masts of the ship.   I myself was carried round by the arms, being grievously sick.   Thereafter we saw the mountain no more, and came to Cyprus on the third Saturday." [1]

We smile at the story, and wonder that a man of undoubted good faith and intelligence could have written it down.   We have been taught by experience to reject the magical value of formulas in the physical

[1] "Memoirs of the Lord of Joinville," p. 56.   A new English version by Ethel Wedgwood.

world. Is it certain that we do not cling to a half-belief in their powers in a higher sphere ? It is surely less superstitious to believe that the good Dean's procession changed the position of a ship in the Mediterranean, than to believe that any outward act in itself can affect the relation of a man's soul to God ; or that spiritual benefit can be obtained by means that are not *in pari materia*. The danger of such superstitious hopes lies for us chiefly in our view of the Sacrament of Holy Communion. We are not to judge that Mystery by the cold light of Reason. It is veiled for us in clouds of reverence and awe. We believe, and we are justified in believing, that there the true worshipper feels a Presence and receives a Gift which are not his but through the Sacrament ; and we need a very strong and delicate sincerity if we would not be tempted to profane the reality and holiness of the thing symbolized, by ascribing a magical virtue to its symbols. Yet if we are to commend the doctrine of God which we profess, we must attain and jealously guard that sincerity. Any teaching which in mistaken reverence gives absolute value to ceremonial acts, is a stumbling-block to honest and intelligent minds, and finds no support in the teaching of our Lord.

In the days of His Flesh He submitted Himself to outward forms of religious observance, and He does not dispense us from them ; for He knew that man is a creature of the senses ; so He gave the service of reverent lip and bent knee their place in the religious life ; but it was the second place : " These ought ye to have done,

and not to have left the other undone." He cleared for
ever from the path of them that seek Him the snare of
intellectual subtleties, when he cried, "I thank Thee,
Father, Lord of heaven and earth, because Thou hast
hid these things from the wise and prudent and revealed
them unto babes."[1] He freed worship from the bondage
of forms and ceremonies by His word: "The hour
cometh when ye shall neither in this mountain nor yet
at Jerusalem worship the Father. . . . God is a spirit,
and they that worship Him must worship Him in spirit
and in truth."[2]

[1] Luke x. 21.   [2] John iv. 21, 24.

LECTURE IV

WAR AND TRADE

"It seems impossible to conceive three things more opposite at first sight to the Sermon on the Mount than War, Law, and Trade; yet Christian society has long since made up its mind about them, and we all accept them as among the necessities or occupations of human society."—DEAN CHURCH.

LECTURE IV

WAR AND TRADE

" Then came also publicans to be baptized, and said unto John, Master, what shall we do? And he said unto them, Exact no more than that which is appointed you. And the soldiers likewise demanded of him saying, And what shall we do? And he said unto them, Do violence to no man, neither accuse any falsely, and be content with your wages."—LUKE iii. 12-14.

1. So far I have spoken chiefly of the message of Christ to the individual soul. I have tried to show that Christianity, as He taught it, is able to satisfy alike the demands of the intelligence and the cravings of the spirit; that it gives a true and sufficient answer to the Riddle of Life ; the only answer that will cover all the facts. I must now pass on to consider the still more difficult problem of the relation of the Gospel to the complex life of highly organized societies. The problem includes three questions : one easy to answer, the other two less easy. First, is existing civilization in harmony with the rule of life laid down by Christ? Second, can it, as it stands, be brought into harmony with that rule ? And third, if the opposition proves to be wholly or in part irreconcilable, which is to give way ?

In this Lecture I propose first to study the modern

State in its relation to other states and communities, reserving till later the consideration of the State's treatment of its own citizens, and their dealings with one another.

The two great external manifestations of national activity are Trade and War. They are so nearly connected that the line between them cannot always be clearly defined, and are in fact two aspects of the same national rivalry. War has commercial prosperity as its aim and as its basis. The Flag has learned to follow Trade. In a practical age wars are mostly fought for markets, and the gigantic cost of armaments has made kings and statesmen more than ever dependent on the help and good will of great financiers. And Trade has all the spirit, and some of the forms of War. The trader does not commonly go forth with drums beating and colours flying, as he did in the great days of the Spanish Main, when there was no peace south of the Line. The age may be past in which our own East India Company and the Netherlands Company were independent polities, with armies and fleets and ambassadors of their own, who treated on equal terms with Eastern princes and commonwealths, or fought them as seemed best in their own eyes, and dealt summarily with interlopers in their seas as pirates and outlaws. But the spirit of the old adventurers is not dead. It is not so long since we saw a Chartered Company levying war in form on its own account. And a strong and ambitious nation is always ready by war, or diplomacy based on the menace of war, to open ports and markets

for its own merchants, or keep them closed against
their rivals, and sometimes to force their commodities
upon unwilling purchasers. And even where there is
no question of armed intervention, Trade is still the
counterpart of War in its merciless dealing with
opponents, its indifference to the welfare of non-
combatants, and its calculated sacrifice of the rank and
file of its own armies in the cause of ultimate success.
Its methods can only be described in metaphors of
battlefield and siege; for it is essentially a truceless
fight for what both sides desire, and only one can
possess.

But there is another side to the picture. If the sole
result of it all was the amassing of a fortune by one
man, or a few men, we might simply deny the value of
the end, and the means would stand condemned with it.
But the question is not so simple. Whatever we may
think of millionaires, we must admit that the making of
one means the employment of a great deal of labour, and
the encouragement of talent and energy. The defenders
of the existing system recognize the evils inherent in
it; but maintain that only on these terms can great
commercial enterprises be built up ; and that the distri-
bution of wealth is governed and governable, not by
moral, but by economic laws. I hope to return later to
this argument, for I am bound to question whether the
desired end be not attainable at a less sacrifice. But for
the present it is sufficient to observe that some of the
maxims of policy and business are admittedly opposed
to the precepts of the Gospel.

2. In the case of War, the opposition would seem at first sight still clearer. In the light of the Sermon on the Mount, it looks as if War could never be necessary or justifiable. And here, at least, there is no disquieting plea from the economists to be met. Huge armaments do indeed employ a vast mass of labour, but at what cost to the commonwealth! In Europe to-day, millions of hands are withdrawn from productive employment, intelligence and scientific ability are largely diverted from beneficent channels, to create and maintain a vast and complicated machinery, which in all probability will never be used at all; and if it is used, is framed solely for the destruction of life and property. The cost of armaments, it is said, and perhaps truly, is a guarantee of peace; but it is a ruinously expensive system of insurance against the self-seeking spirit which is alleged to be the mainspring of all enterprise. And if War, and the preparation for War, are clumsy and wasteful methods of attaining their professed purpose, still less, it would appear, can they be reconciled with the teaching of Christ. "Thou shalt not kill," is a plain command; it is confirmed and extended in the Sermon on the Mount, and the enunciation of the *lex talionis* in the Mosaic Law is met and annulled with "But I say unto you, resist not the evil." Is not the command plain and absolute? The servants of the Kingdom which is not of this world must not fight. The Quaker position is the only honest and reasonable position. But in fact, the question is, as we know very well, not so simple. In the first place, we must clear away a

great deal of prejudice and sentiment which cluster round it and seem to belong to it, but will be found on examination to be quite irrelevant. We must make quite certain that the objections we feel to war are really Christian.

We can all remember the shock of horror, almost of astonishment, which ran through the Press and the public mind in this country, when the first reports came that men were being killed in considerable numbers in the South African War. It was a salutary shock; because it brought home to us what had been long forgotten, the true cost and misery of War, and dashed our light-hearted illusions with a cold touch of reality. A keen emotion, as yet not dulled by use, at the thought that men had died for their country, and that English homes were mourning for their loss, was the better part of the impulse that disturbed our complacency; but it had baser elements than pity and sympathy. It is an ungracious task to analyze sentiments which make men gentler and more merciful; but I think it needs to be said that the exaggerated respect for human life, which is a distinctive note of our own age as compared with all previous history, is not in itself a Christian feeling. It is due partly, no doubt, to the greater security with which good government and efficient police surround us. We are not accustomed to see men killed; and therefore we have come to think violent death a more dreadful thing than our fathers thought it: more dreadful, perhaps, than it really is. But a deeper cause of the tremendous value we put on life, and our corresponding

terror of sudden death, is our waning faith in immortality ; and, what seems to me more serious, a waning
faith in the value of spiritual things as against material.
We allow ourselves to be cowed and shaken by a half
belief, that if you kill a man there is an end of him in
every way ; an end of action, an end of happiness.   If
you take away his bodily life, you take away everything.
Happily, it is only a half belief.   It may be unassailable
in logic ; but men very commonly do not act upon it
when it comes to the pinch.   They throw their lives
away for fifty things whereof the value cannot be
worked out in terms of earthly pleasure or profit ; and
the higher part of our nature honours and justifies their
action.   But if such a belief were far stronger on
grounds of experience than it is, it is profoundly and
essentially unchristian.   The Christian is taught to hold
life very lightly in the balance with what is eternal.
One great part—if not truly the whole—of our Lord's
work was the changing of values ; and this change of
value is the very centre of His teaching by precept and
example.   "He that findeth his life shall lose it, and he
that loseth his life for My sake shall find it." [1]   It is
not even necessary to accept the doctrine of personal
immortality in order to receive this teaching : that
the true value of life lies, not in retaining it at all costs
as a "permanent possibility of sensation ;" but in using it
and losing it, if need be, in the cause of Righteousness.

But, after all, we must return to the plain commands, "Thou shalt not kill," "Resist not the evil."

[1] Matt. x. 39.

There they stand for us to take or leave ; but if we choose to leave them, we have no right to call ourselves disciples of Christ.   The danger of weakening or explaining away plain commands is great.   But there is another danger : the danger of taking isolated texts and disregarding all else.   We must read Christ's words in their immediate context, and in their connection with His whole teaching.   Dr. Gore points out, in his "Commentary on the Sermon on the Mount," that the words "Resist not the evil" are spoken to the individual believer ; and, from the individual, they demand absolute and unqualified obedience ; but they do not exclude corporate action for the repression of wrong, which is actually commanded in a later passage in this same collection of our Lord's sayings.   The distinction is not in the commentary, but in the Text.

"We observe," he writes, "two opposite duties. There is the clear duty, so far as mere personal feeling goes, of simple self-effacement.   Only then, when we have got our wills thoroughly subordinated to God's will, when all the wild instinct of revenge is subdued, are we in a position to consider the other duty, and to ask ourselves what the maintenance of the moral order of society may require of us." [1]

The duty of interference is secondary and derivative. It can properly be exercised only by those who fulfil the individual duty; the hope of awakening the dormant conscience of Society lies far less in any external pressure, than in the moral power of lives in

[1] 1904 edition, pp. 85, 86.

which the spirit of personal resentment and reprisal has been subdued ; and, that pressure being external, its use is temporary in proportion to its success, and ceases to be, when it has accomplished its purpose ; it is a proof and confession of imperfection ; but while society is imperfect, moral discipline is necessary ; and must be enforced, if need be, by the sharpest sanctions. If the world were Christian, there would be no War and no need of War ; but in a world that is slowly becoming Christian, War is not the worst thing we see, nor the first to be abolished. So long as men live by the principles of selfishness, a just war will often be, not only inevitable, but better than ignoble peace ; and so long as War is necessary, it will be most mercifully carried on by strict adherence to its own stern rules. The General or the Nation that tries to mingle peace with war, is like the surgeon whose hand falters in pity, and so prolongs the misery he thinks to palliate.

In this connection we may observe that Jesus Himself did not anticipate the speedy cessation of War, nor denounce War as such ; indeed, in His comment on the Sixth Commandment He virtually draws the distinction which our conscience feels to exist between War and Murder ; it is not the act of slaying, but the spirit of murder, hatred, and revenge, which He condemns. The distinction is for us a matter of very delicate casuistry in practice, and can easily be attacked in theory *ratione ruentis acervi* ; but it exists. It is more than habit which makes us hold that there is a moral difference between killing a man in battle,

and killing the same man from motives of greed or
revenge.   This belief finds strong support in the good
effects which War has on moral character.   Some men
it brutalizes and hardens, but the Christian soldier is
a familiar and genuine type.   It is good for most of
us to be brought face to face with hardship and the
peril of death; and the discipline of War sometimes
produces, not only the admirable virtue of courage,
but qualities still more precious, obedience, loyalty,
self-sacrifice, and even tenderness, in a greater degree
than the routine of Peace.   The ideal of Chivalry is
not wholly fanciful.   I will borrow a poet's description
of what Chivalry seemed to the noblest of those who
saw it, and loved it in its prime.

"Let me understand you," said Stephen.   "Chivalry
as I have seen it from a distance, I have taken to
mean a love of fighting, a love of pageantry, and a
fantastic love of women, mixed into a rather unwhole-
some ferment."

"You have lived abroad," replied Lord Bryan;
"there is no place in England for that kind of folly,
and so far as I know there never has been.   For us
Chivalry is a plain rule of conduct, by which a man
may live in a world of men, without savagery and
without monkery."

"Good!" exclaimed Stephen; "but how?"

"Look at the Prince," said Lord Bryan; "it is
written large in him.   He is pious and courteous, the
brother of all brave men, the servant of the weak,
the beaten, and the suffering.   In short, he loves God

with all his heart, and his neighbour as himself.   What is that ? "

" That is Christianity ; but I ask you again, how does loving your neighbour come to include fighting him or taking his life ? "

" I reply with another question.   Are you not confusing the unreal with the real—putting the material before the spiritual ?   The warfare of every one of us must end in death; we need not love a man less because it falls to us to strike the final stroke; it is only the hatred, the treachery, the selfishness that make the crime of murder; and what injury can the real man suffer except those inflicted by himself ? " [1]

3. We should conclude, then, that no sweeping judgment, either of approval or condemnation, can be passed on War as a whole.   Like Civil Justice, it is a terrible remedy, and it behoves those who use it to have a clear conscience and clean hands.   Yet, like all inflictions of pain, it may be salutary.   But if it is used wantonly, or for wrong and selfish ends, it is abominable and unpardonable.   And it has too often been used both wantonly and selfishly.   Fighting was the chief business and amusement of the upper classes of Europe in the Middle Ages, and that Chivalry, which gave such romantic grace and dignity to noble life, had a very ugly side.   The delicate consideration of knight for knight took little account of the churl.   We read of Edward the Black Prince, that after Poitiers—

" When the French King was first brought to him,

[1] "The Old Country," by Henry Newbolt, p. 304.

he offered, quite naturally and simply, to help him off
with his armour.   The King said with great dignity,
' Thank you, cousin, but after this it is not for you
to serve me ; no Prince has ever won such honour in
a single day.'   The Prince was touched to the quick,
he cannot bear that his honour should be another's
misfortune.   He said in a very low voice, ' God forgive
me this victory.' " [1]

We admire the Prince's exquisite and sincere
humility and courtesy to his royal prisoner, but I
wonder what the French peasants of the time thought
of the Black Prince.   They were outside the rules of
the Great Game, and were harried alternately, without
mercy or remedy, by their own forces and by the enemy.

Chivalry, as an organized system, is dead ; but the
baser part of it still lives in Militarism, the spirit
which admires War for War's sake, and in some
countries gives the Army the privilege of despising
and looking down on the civilian and the worker.
That spirit has never been congenial to the English
character.   The bitter lesson of the short military
tyranny of Cromwell has saved us from that danger
till now ; but it is a danger, and when we are told that
the one thing needful in the education of a Christian
boy is that he should be trained to kill his fellow-
creatures with skill and certainty, we begin to have
ground for uneasiness.

Yet among the causes which have tempted men
to aggressive wars, a pure love of fighting is the rarest,

" The Old Country," p. 299.

and perhaps the most respectable, and in nearly every
case some more solid gain has been the object.   In old
days kings fought for glory and territory; either
in pursuance of an alleged right like Edward III.,
or in cynical disregard of all rights like Louis XIV.
Or the motive might be the desire to divert to other
fields energies which were growing unmanageable at
home.   So it was when Chichele counselled Henry V.
to make the War of Agincourt.   So Napoleon III. was
lured into a conflict with Germany in 1870.   So, we
are told, Russia lately provoked Japan, as a last hope
of preventing or deferring Revolution.   But these are
causes which influence kings and statesmen, and, as I
suggested above, it is not kings and statesmen any longer
who have the last word in the policy of nations, but
financiers.   We grow more and more practical; and
War that was the mistress of Princes, has fallen to be
the handmaid of Commerce.   And of such a war as
that it is a ticklish thing to speak.   We are too near
one; and with the most scrupulous care I shall be
fortunate indeed if I offend none.

> " Periculosae plenum opus aleae
> Tentabo, et incedam per ignes
> Suppositos cineri doloso."

At least experience has taught us that a Nation does
well to be sure it knows what it is fighting for, before
it takes the field, and to weigh well the magnitude
of the task it has undertaken, and the sacrifices which
will have to be made before the end.   So much perhaps
we are agreed upon; but we are not agreed upon the

question of the right attitude of a great commercial
Empire to less civilized peoples on its borders.   It is
a question which our position in the world forces us
to answer as a Nation ; one which as investors many
of us are under obligation to answer to our consciences.
And in those cases where the attractions of profitable
speculation are plainly on one side, and Christian duty
on the other, it takes some moral courage to answer
it sincerely.   We may be justly convinced that we
are able to improve the resources of a country to better
effect than its native inhabitants either can or will ;
but it does not follow that we have therefore a right
to expropriate them, either by summary process of arms,
or by the slower and more degrading extinction that
befalls a savage race which is brought in contact with
the vices and distempers of civilization.   It is at least
clear that for a society or an individual claiming the
name of Christian, there must be no War of aggression
for the sake of gain, either under the forms of War
or under the forms of Trade.   Only extreme necessity
and the strictest purity of motive can justify War ;
but it appears that there are circumstances in which
a Christian Society is not only permitted but compelled
to apply to moral evil the drastic surgery of pain and
death, if it plainly cannot be cured otherwise.

> οὐ πρὸς ἰατροῦ σοφοῦ
> θρηνεῖν ἐπῳδὰς πρὸς τομῶντι πήματι.[1]

4. And if the violent remedy of War be ever
allowable, it should be easy by comparison to bring

[1] Sophocles, "Ajax," 582.

within the Rule of the Gospel the peaceful and beneficent activities of Manufacture and Commerce which
put the gifts of Nature at the service of man.   But
as a matter of experience we find that here Christianity
is more frankly excluded, and that, not only by those
who are directly interested — merchants, speculators,
investors, and the like—but by others, who do not
gain, but rather suffer by its exclusion ; and, strangest
of all, by many who profess and practise Christianity
in their private lives.   There appears to be a general
consent, the more powerful in practice that it is seldom
expressed in words, that Christian morals have no
place in Business.   Such an attitude is quite intelligible for those whose one idea of the purpose of business
is buying cheap and selling dear, and so making the
largest possible profit ; but it is shared by people who
have no selfish end to serve by it, and who sincerely
dislike oppression and dishonesty.

May I, without seeming censorious, take a concrete
instance ?   It has been a common experience of late,
when a certain much controverted expedient has been
under discussion, to hear the question settled by the
plea that "the gold cannot be extracted otherwise."
The point to notice is that quite good men regarded
that argument as final.   But just consider it for a
moment in the light of Christ's teaching on Riches.
One cause of this state of mind is undoubtedly a false
estimate of the importance of being rich.   But another,
and I think a more fundamental cause is a wrong
conception of Christianity and its sphere.

"As long as Christianity is content with what you call humble aims, that is to say, as long as it is willing to be regarded merely as the dogma of an established sect which is not to interfere with the movements of human society at all, which is to leave it to regulate itself upon the most selfish tyrannical hateful maxims, and only to prevent the sufferers from disturbing its movements; so long the most vague dreams of fancy which have a show of freedom, or the most terrible despotism which has a show of government, will be preferred to it."[1]

These disquieting words of Frederick Denison Maurice are, thank God, a shade less applicable to us to-day than when they were spoken; for they have done some of their work in awaking the Christian conscience; but what they have done is little compared with what they have yet to do before we get Religion into its right place in the national life. And if their purpose has been in some measure fulfilled, their warning is more abundantly fulfilled. The " terrible despotism which has a show of government" is realized in the great commercial monopolies which we call Trusts. The Trusts are useful in a way which their promoters probably do not contemplate. They have proved that Combination is stronger than Competition, and have invented and perfected an organization which may be used for very different ends. What groups of men have done for their own advantage and profit, Society can do for the profit and advantage of all.

---

[1] "Christian Socialism," by F. D. Maurice.

Meanwhile the system has made the Middleman, the
manufacturer and distributor, absolute master of the
producer, the workman, and the consumer, with what
results to these classes we know. And in revenge,
the few who reap the gigantic profits do not seem to
get much good of them. It looks as if there were a
Law of Nature, perhaps a Law of God, which prevents
any single man from rightly enjoying or using monstrous
wealth. After all, there is a limit to the pleasurable
spending of money on the most costly and ingenious
forms of self-indulgence; and when the hugely rich try to
divert some portion of their swollen gains to benefit the
fellow-creatures they have exploited, they are not very
successful; their excursions into philanthropy are apt
to be mischievous or absurd: there is, as old-fashioned
people would say, no blessing on it. The French
Crusader, whose book I have mentioned before, has a
word so much in point that I cannot refrain from
quoting it—

"The Devil," he says, "is so cunning about it, that
in the case of great usurers and robbers, he wiles them
into giving to God that which they ought to *restore* to
its owners." [1]

5. In this country we have not yet had full experience of the effects of monopolies; we are still suffering
rather from the evils of unregulated competition. Of
these evils we are all becoming acutely conscious,
though we are not at all agreed on the right means
for remedying them. The under-payment of certain

---

[1] "Memoirs of the Lord of Joinville," p. 15.

classes of labour is apparently inevitable under strict
economic laws, yet it is an intolerable evil, scandalous
in itself, but still more dreadful in its effects upon the
physical and moral condition of future generations. It is
gradually coming to be recognized that it is the interest
of the employer to pay his workers something more
than a bare subsistence wage—what we may call a self-
respect wage ; but this motive operates hitherto chiefly
in trades where the workers are able to combine and
help themselves. There are other classes of workers
with whom this is *not* the immediate interest of the
employer. It pays him better to give them a wage
that will just keep them able to work for a few years,
and when they break down, to take others in their
place. This is the case just in those trades where the
employer's profit is small, so that he is under strong
temptation to save where he can ; and where it is not
possible for the workers to combine and protect themselves by a standard rate of wages ; and where, if one
rebels or falls out, there are plenty of others ready to
take the work and the starvation pay.

We see in the condition of unorganized and casual
labour in our great cities the most striking form of
the evil, but it is not confined to them. The relation
of Capital to Labour everywhere is strained and un-
satisfactory, and will continue to be so, so long as they
are regarded and regard themselves as enemies, trying
to get the better of each other. The only permanent
solution lies in an alliance of Capital and Labour,
which will give to the worker a direct interest in the

⸱ccess and efficiency of the enterprise in which he is
engagᵊ⸍

Most of u⸍ have not a direct connection with the
employment of labᵘᵘ⸍ on a large scale, and we may
persuade ourselves that great industrial questions are
beyond our powers of understanding or interference,
and therefore do not involve either responsibility or
personal interest for us; but there is a relation in
which we are all forced into contact with Trade, and
are all affected by the state of commercial morality,
and affect it in turn—the relation of Buyer and Seller.
We may read reports in the papers of Trade Disputes,
of Strikes and Lock-outs, statistics of unemployment,
even accounts of terrible poverty and degradation,
without feeling that they touch us very nearly; but
it is a different tale when we find that we have not
bought, perhaps cannot buy, what we intended to pay
for; that we have been cheated by a skilfully drawn
misstatement of the quality or origin of goods that we
have purchased; when a deliberately scamped bit of
plumbing has brought sickness or death into our household; when we discover that the loyalty of our servants
has been bought away from us by a pushing tradesman,
with bribes that ultimately come out of our own
pockets.   The adulteration of food probably falls
hardest on the very poor, who have little margin of
choice, and are obliged to take what they can get from
the shops where they must deal, and is therefore a
most serious evil in its effects on the physique of our
toilers.   But dishonest workmanship and bribery affect

all classes alike, and the welfare of the Nation as a
whole more seriously than that of any single class.   A
Committee of the London Chamber of Commerce nine
years ago reported that—

"Secret Commissions in various forms are prevalent
in almost all trades and professions to a great extent,
and that in some trades the practice has increased, and
is increasing." [1]

And since then this evil has been considered great
enough to call for legislative action.   It is probably
true, as we are told on good authority, that, "speaking
generally, men who transact business to a fairly large
extent, or who enjoy a practical monopoly, as owning a
well-established trade with an assured amount of custom,
are more or less distinguishable from those who occupy
various positions in the descending scale." [2]

But it is not universally true.   Even the great
Houses are sometimes driven by the stress of competition to methods which no honest man would contemplate in his personal dealings.   It is not an unheard-of
thing that an engineering firm of standing and repute
should cut the Government stamp out of girders which
had been passed by the Inspector, and let it into
inferior, or, at any rate, untested stuff.   The audacity
of the fraud and its cruelty—for the soundness of a
girder may mean the lives of many men—give it a
bad pre-eminence ; but it is caused and excused by the

---

[1] Report adopted by the Chamber, July 7, 1898.

[2] "Commericial Morality," by the Rev. H. S. Holland and the
Rev. J. Carter, p. 3.

same reasons as the obtaining of contracts by influence or bribery, which appears, by what comes out from time to time, to be a common thing. Custom of the trade emerges on all sides as a hindrance to honest work and impartial dealing. Every part of the fabric of Commerce seems to be tainted with one of these three plagues—adulteration, misrepresentation, bribery. It is an ugly indictment. But we are not justified in saying that business men, contractors, tradesmen, are wickeder than other people, or even wickeder than we are. "Think ye that they are sinners above all men? I tell you, Nay: but, except ye repent, ye shall all likewise perish."[1] In fact, *we* are the great sinners; the men who cheat us, and oppress the labourer, are the victims partly of our faults as well as of their own. If this is not immediately apparent, let us consider the three following propositions :—

First, "Most of the tricks and immoralities of trade are due to the increasing stress of competition." Second, "It is the ordinary consumer who is largely to blame for this excessive competition, through the prevailing passion for cheap bargains." And third, "The responsibility of deciding how trade should be carried on lies upon the conscience and intelligence of the general public."[2]

This passion for cheapness must not be dignified by the name of thrift. Thrift is to abstain from buying things we cannot afford. The passion for cheapness arises either from the desire—generally, one is glad

[1] Luke xiii. 4, 5.   [2] "Commercial Morality," p. 5.

to think, disappointed—to get more than we pay for ;
or from the still meaner wish to seem richer than
we are.   And if we do succeed in our bargain, succeed
in stealing some part of the true price of what we
buy, still it has to be paid for, dearly, thrice over ;
paid for in our own loss of honesty and self-respect,
in the suffering of fellow-creatures, in the demoraliza-
tion of Trade.   And yet, once more, it is paid for in a
very practical way ; for a forced and artificial cheapness
kills good work, and drives out genuine commodities.
When we have indulged ourselves for a little while in
buying an inferior substitute cheap, we find we cannot
buy the real thing we wanted either dear or cheap.

We have tried Competition to the full, and it has
made life into an unending struggle : nothing so respectable as a real War, with its clear issues and
definite results ; but rather like the aimless, murderous
bickerings of savage tribes, which give to the strong
hand for a moment more than its share, at the cost
of infinite material waste, suffering, and moral degradation.   Those who have suffered most in the past have
learned the lesson—that in co-operation, the sacrifice
of a part of the individual claim, lies their strength.
Trade unions are not faultless ; they have had their
mistakes, even their crimes ; their spokesmen are apt
to be self-assertive and inconsiderate ; but they had,
and still have, a long account to make up before the
balance is even ; and if we consider the state of Labour
from which they sprang, the work they have done
hitherto must be reckoned wholly for good.

And now the day of power has dawned for the labouring classes, and with power comes danger. If they return evil for evil, and in their turn exact more than is their due ; if they use their strength for oppression and injustice, if they try to outlaw the capitalist, and the employer, and their own uncovenanted brethren, they will not only fail of their purpose, but they will fall hopeless and unregretted like other tyrannies before them. But if they resolve to carry out the Law of Co-operation with justice and mercy, they have a better hope than kings and priests have ever had ; they are nearer to Christ, because they have been poor and despised and oppressed. But it is the Spirit of Christ alone that can bring the great work to accomplishment. Self-interest has proved itself too weak and short-sighted a motive to make men work together for good. There is nothing but a belief in the Fatherhood of God and the Oneness of men with Him and in Him that can make us think of others and treat them as brethren, seeing our good in their good. And the thought of the Fatherhood of God takes away the great motive of selfish competition. Because He is our Father, we need not be troubled about the necessaries of life—what we shall eat, and what we shall drink, and wherewithal we shall be clothed. Which commandment and promise certainly do not mean that we are to sit with folded hands and vacant minds ; but that, if we are doing our work in the world, we shall have enough, and need not and must not be anxious about more. If we could learn and teach these two

lessons of the Fatherhood of God, to care for others
and to put away over-care for ourselves; a good many
economic problems would be solved by ceasing to
exist.   We need not *then* despair of seeing, what
sounds so impossible, so absurd to-day, every class
in the commonwealth fulfilling the function for which
it is really fitted, which it alone can properly fulfil,
pursuing not its own interest, but the interest of its
correlative; the employer seeing to it that Labour has
a fair wage and wholesome conditions; the Trade
Union exacting from its members a good day's work;
the buyer insisting on prices that are just to the workman and the seller ; while the seller takes care that the
buyer gets what he pays for in good measure.   It is
the vision of a Trade Utopia, yet not beyond realization
—if men were Christians.

H

LECTURE V

SOCIAL QUESTIONS

" A stern discouragement of the accumulation of wealth, except as held consciously on trust for the public good; a strenuous opposition to the development of luxury as distinct from knowledge and beauty; a constant practical realization of the temper of contentment, with sufficient and wholesome food and lodgement, air and clothing, work and leisure, and of the greater blessing of giving as compared with receiving."— GORE.

LECTURE V

"But Jesus called them unto Him, and said, Ye know that the princes of the Gentiles exercise dominion over them, and they that are great exercise authority upon them. But it shall not be so among you: but whosoever will be great among you, let him be your minister; and whosoever will be chief among you, let him be your servant: even as the Son of Man came not to be ministered unto, but to minister."—MATT. xx. 25-28.

1. AN objection is commonly taken to the teaching of Jesus as a rule of life on the ground that it is anti-social, or at least ignores the social problems which are our chief trouble and our chief interest at the present day. It is pointed out that a general and literal observance of certain precepts which are of the essence of His teaching in the Sermon on the Mount would mean the dissolution of the social order as it exists. There is the precept of boundless generosity: "Give to him that asketh of thee, and from him that would borrow of thee turn not thou away;" [1] the precept of absolute non-resistance to physical, legal, and official violence: "Whosoever shall smite thee on the right cheek, turn to him the other also. If any man will sue thee at the law, and take away thy coat, let him

[1] Matt. v. 42.

have thy cloke also.   And whosoever shall compel thee to go a mile, go with him twain." [1]

Such maxims as these strike right across the ideas of property, discipline, and the personal rights of the citizen, on which our civilization is founded; and, in fact, no one, or hardly any one, attempts to obey them literally.   But it does not follow that they are to be rejected forthwith as impracticable.   The divine paradox claims our attention by its inconsistency with our practice, and with the principles which we are accustomed to accept as axioms of social conduct.

Without going to the length of maintaining that whenever the laws of Society appear to conflict with any single utterance of our Lord, they must at once be rejected by Christians, we may inquire how far the complications we are trying to unravel, spring from self-assertion, and from an extreme insistence on rights which, in their time, were as undisputed as those which we value so highly; and we shall find that social codes at the best have no permanent or absolute authority to justify a rigid application, but can only be worked, for good, by a large measure of concession and self-effacement.   And when we turn from history to what we can really best judge, our own life and character, it becomes apparent that hardly any degree of self-discipline in this direction is exaggerated or unnecessary.   We must be singularly different from the common race of men, or singularly dull, if we do not realize that our actions and thoughts are governed

[1] Matt. v. 39–41.

by a jealous sense of property, a relentless insistence on personal rights and personal dignity, which are injurious alike to our own moral development, and to our usefulness as members of a society. We are so far from the just mean in our value for ourselves and for others, that the danger of the opposite extreme is, for the present, hardly worth considering. Our Lord's teaching corresponds to the fact. He does but show a knowledge of our nature, teaching in proverbs, short absolute commands, which press the claim of the duty most flagrantly neglected, to the exclusion of all else for the moment, but only for the moment. He who came to teach every man his duty to God, his neighbour, and himself, does not forget social justice ; but it is only those who have conquered pride and selfishness in themselves who can safely discipline others.

2. The teaching of Jesus is intensely, almost exclusively, practical ; it touches every part of daily life, and can only be fully carried out by those who are living and working in the world, those for whom it was intended. But for all that, Jesus was not what we call a Social Reformer ; He does not give us rules for dealing directly with the social problems of to-day. He did not deal directly with the social and industrial problems of His own time, and seems to have taken little interest in them. He accepted civil Government as it stood, whether Roman or Jewish, without desire to change or criticize it. The judge, the officer, the jailer, are forces to be reckoned with ; and they are more than

that—they are the representatives of justice. He has no detailed commands for us on economic questions, nor, what seems stranger still to us, on Slavery. The merchant, the soldier, the publican, master and servant, are taken as parts of the existing system. They are not separate types to Him ; each is no more and no less than a human soul. Doubtless the cause of this indifference is partly to be found in the conditions of our Lord's human life and consciousness. Not that here He simply accepted, as He so often does, the opinions and beliefs of His country and generation ; on the contrary, He is strikingly out of sympathy with the political hopes and passions of the Jews of His time. He would not be the Messiah they wanted ; and His refusal inspired the spirit of submission to the civil power, which was a most valuable protection to the early Church.

But whatever we may think of the limits of His foreknowledge, we must admit that He produced in the minds of His immediate disciples a belief that the World was destined speedily to pass away, and that therefore the amending of its institutions was not a business which demanded the thought and care of the Christian. In the short time which remained before the Second Coming there was other work for him to do—the reformation of his own soul, the care of the brethren, and the preaching of the Gospel. So much we may admit ; but it does not follow that we have here the whole explanation of Christ's attitude to social questions. If our Lord's teaching does not anywhere

coincide with modern theories of social reform, it is
because it transcends them in either direction. It is
at once more universal and more particular. It is
more particular because it takes as its subject, as the
unit to be dealt with, not a nation, a class, or a trade,
but the single soul in its relation to God and its
neighbour.

"His work was to awake the individual to love
and to make the individual realize his responsibility
towards his brother; and thus Jesus did a work which
beyond all others was for eternity; and still to-day
He calls us back from the distracting maze of pro-
grammes and panaceas for the reform of the world,
to the reform of our own selves, which is the reform
which is chiefly needed." [1]

And His teaching is at the same time more universal
in that He does not deal with particular cases, but
with the Law of Character. As we read in St. Luke's
Gospel, " One of the company said unto Him, Master,
speak to my brother, that he divide the inheritance
with me. And He said unto him, Man, who made Me
a judge or a divider over you? And He said unto
them, Take heed, and beware of covetousness : for a
man's life consisteth not in the abundance of the things
which he possesseth." [2]

He will not deal with the particular dispute : that
is the business of the Magistrate ; but He gives the
Rule which governs all such cases, and is to guide the

[1] P. Wernle, "Beginnings of Christianity," vol. i. p. 82.
[2] Luke xii. 13–15.

whole thought and action of the disciples with regard
to property. This is the great principle which dis-
tinguishes our Lord's treatment of evil from so much
of our attempts. He deals with evil as He deals with
disease ; not by treating symptoms, particular outward
manifestations, but by reaching and healing the root
of the mischief. And this is why He does not always
satisfy us. The disinherited brother would have been
better pleased if the Master had given sentence that
he should have half the estate, but neither he nor
his brother would have been better. The division of
the property was a small thing; done grudgingly and
with resentment, it would have been a bad thing : it
was the spirit of generosity that mattered.

Our Lord's precepts on these difficult subjects may
be likened to the Laws of Health. They are broad
and simple and natural. But to disregard them not
only brings punishment and death, but makes the
laws themselves for the time of none effect. The
organism once depraved and diseased cannot return
to obey and profit by the simple rules that guide
the healthy creature, except by long and painful
discipline. Therefore *our* study of social problems is
to be compared to Pathology and Morbid Anatomy,
but with a difference. The doctor takes the diseased
state as his starting-point to cure it; all his interest
for the moment is centred on it—its symptoms, its
phases, and its origin. But his whole purpose, even
if meanwhile he treats symptoms in order to spare
the patient suffering, is to remove the cause of the

distemper and restore the body to a state of health.
And in this the Christian social reformer imitates him,
and differs from all who hope to cure the disorders
of the State without Christianity; by which I mean,
in this place, strictly the teaching of Christ.   All
attempts at reform which are based on the acceptance
of Selfishness, enlightened or unenlightened, as the
sole motive of action, seem to me to take the cause
of the disease, the disease itself, as the normal and
permanent state, and to base their treatment on the
principle not of its removal, but of its continuance.
They propose, by a skilful treatment of symptoms, to
convert the poison of disease into the principle of
healthy life ; or, to put it in other terms, they hope
to educate and tame the root-spirit of strife and greed,
till it becomes an instrument of order and righteousness.
There is no hope that way.   That law of Social
Progress is bound to lead us back in a vicious circle
to its starting-point—the interest of the stronger.   The
only possible alternative to Christianity is a profound
and reasonable pessimism.

3. In the face of that alternative we are forced to
admit that, after nineteen hundred years of Christianity, whatever may be the case with individuals,
Society at present is certainly not Christian ; not
Christian in its aims and methods, not Christian in
its judgments.   There is no more striking instance
of the opposition than the value it sets upon riches
and poverty.   We are awakening, as I have said
above, to the importance of the labouring classes, not

only as a political power, but as our brethren, who
have a claim to our love and understanding; and
yet I think I am not wrong in saying that we regard
them still as what we call them—the lower classes,
vessels made to dishonour in the great household of
the State, doing the drudgery of life for us, and fit
only for drudgery. Poverty is a reproach, at any
rate a thing evil in itself, which a man is justified in
stretching a point or two to escape, for himself and
for those who belong to him. We keep honour for
intellect and culture, accounting them the elements
which vivify the dull mass. To Christ it seemed
otherwise. If we may judge His mind from His
words and His life, the Poor, for Him, hold a very
different place in society. They represent not the
dull and mechanical members, but the spiritual part
of man's being; while intellect and culture stand for
the mind and the senses; they have a place, but it
is not the highest place. The highest blessing is for
the poor; they are blessed as the natural heirs of
the Kingdom of Heaven, which is not a dim and
future Paradise, but the knowledge and fellowship of
God here and now. And we know that the Perfect
Life, which alone of all human lives was lived in the
full knowledge and fellowship of God, was a life of
stern poverty and hardship, of hunger and thirst:
the Son of Man had not where to lay His Head.

Now if we can bring ourselves to accept His value
of poverty and riches instead of our own, it must very
seriously influence both our opinions and our actions.

We shall not be tempted by a profane travesty of
His words, "The poor ye have always with you," to
let things go their way; but the new value will nevertheless modify considerably our conception of true
philanthropic work. We shall not consider that we
have done all our duty by a poor man as soon as he
is mentally and materially equipped for making himself
rich; for we shall feel that he may be just as badly
off rich as he was poor. And if he is, then so may
we be. And this possibility we must gravely consider.
It is no mere monkish fancy that some men are called
to embrace a life of real poverty for their soul's sake.
And if our conscience does not bid us do that—for
there is room in the Kingdom for the rich as well as
the poor, though their entrance be harder—we shall
at least have a new and strict estimate of necessity
and luxury in personal expenditure, and a very scrupulous care of the disposal of what remains over, that
it may do good and not harm. That is a real difficulty.
If the spiritual part of a man is starved and degraded,
it is ill with his whole being; the intellect and the
senses grow at first proud and tyrannical, but in no
long time they too suffer, and become barren and
dissatisfied. But it is not well either, if the spiritual
part is pampered by asceticism, or drugged with superstition. And as it is with the man, so it is with the
State. The Roman mob, given its food and its amuse-
ments without desert or effort, is not a more wholesome
element in Society than an East End population which,
by dull and exhausting toil, can earn very little food,

and no amusement. There is a real danger in all hasty and ill-considered attempts to relieve distress ; the danger that while we feed the hungry and clothe the naked we may rob them of honesty and self-respect. But that does not mean that we are to make no effort ; it means more effort—the very hard and distasteful effort to understand the evils on which our comfort and our prosperity are based. Have we ever considered what the under-side of the social machine, which serves our purpose on the whole so well, looks like to thousands of our fellow-creatures for whom Christ died ? We are sometimes told that a wealthy society must be based upon extreme poverty and degradation, that the processes necessary to its maintenance cannot be worked without a certain amount of human waste and débris. It may be true. At any rate most of us practically take it pretty much for granted. But supposing we examine such a proposition in the light of Christ's teaching ; suppose we go further and admit that, in London for instance, the highest spiritual potentialities lie, as He thought they lay, in the Poor ; that without them the community cannot be His disciples in any full sense, what answer can we make either to our Master or to our accusers ? He accounted the preaching of the Gospel to the poor the highest part, the most notable mark of His work on earth. The poor of London have been thrust, and are kept by a Society which till lately called itself Christian, in conditions of life which make the preaching of the Gospel to them a mockery. They are practically denied their share in the Fatherhood of God, which, for one thing, promises to honest work enough of the necessities of life. They are always anxious for the morrow with too good cause. They are forced to be dishonest, and impure, and cruel to one another. And the one thing which could save them, the love of Christ, is withheld from them, because they think it is the Creed of those who oppress them. The physical sufferings of the poor—cold, and hunger, and nakedness —are such as may well make the comfortable classes shudder to think of them; but these are not the unpardonable wrong that Society inflicts upon them, for these do not separate from God: it is the moral degradation, the spiritual hardening of these our brethren that is the deadly evil, the burning reproach to a Christian Civilization. I have spoken of London as a typical and familiar example, but it is not in London only, or in other great towns only, that men and women are forced to live like the beasts, without the beast's happy want of self-consciousness. Things have not wholly altered in our English villages, so picturesque and innocent looking, since Charles Kingsley wrote in his poem, "The Poacher's Widow," of the peasant—

> "Worse housed than your hacks and your pointers,
>   Worse fed than your pigs and your sheep."

And then follow the lines which, as you remember, Lancelot Smith would not read, and which I shall not read either, for they touch the difficulty, the impossibility, for English lads and girls of growing up pure in mind and body in the dwellings which Society considers good enough for them.

We marvel that Christ says nothing about Slavery; we are surprised, and a little scandalized, that St. Paul seems to accept it among the institutions of his time without protest. We rightly pride ourselves that the national conscience will not tolerate such an abuse; and that there is no Slavery, or not very much, under the British Flag. But what, if we look at it sincerely, are the conditions of casual and under-paid labour but Slavery without its safeguards? The acknowledged slave was often well treated, clothed and fed, and even maintained in his old age. It was the owner's interest on the whole to keep his human chattels in good condition, and in good temper. The free workers, slaves of penury, have not even the value of a chattel; they are absolutely dependent on employers, who too often cannot afford to treat them well, being themselves in bondage to the tyrant Competition. They cannot leave their miserable work, or if they do wander away, it is only to find elsewhere conditions equally cruel and degrading; they have no claim on their masters, beyond a minimum payment for tasks actually done, and when they fall, weary and worn out, only destitution awaits them. Even the last and vilest reproach of the slave system is not done away: virtue, honour, purity, are as hard to keep for thousands of free women as they were for the veriest slave.

The picture is dark, but I think it is not overdrawn;

and looking on it, let us pause to ask ourselves what, in the face of such facts, is the duty of the State and of the Individual. The individual Christian's duty is hard enough, but it is the easier of the two. We can at least resolve that we will not, if we can help it, take enjoyment or profit out of the degradation of our fellows ; that we will know something of the wants and feelings of those who minister to our ease ; and then, adding love to knowledge, we may hope on a small scale to do good and not harm. The task of the State is infinitely puzzling and dangerous ; there are such huge arrears to make up, and the evil has been allowed to grow so complicated, with roots and offshoots in the most unexpected places. Much may be done, and cries out to be done, in the way of improving material conditions, proper housing, fresh air and water, and the like ; much, again, in regulating trade and employment, seeing that men act honestly, so far as Law, efficiently administered, can make them. But before all things, our counsellers must keep in mind that no permanent reform can be effected by dead lift.

It is not enough to give people subsistence, or even comfort, unless we can give them back, what we have robbed from them, honesty, and self-respect, and the fear of God. The real question of the unemployed, for instance, is not to find them wages, or to find them work, but to re-create in them, what they have lost, the desire to work and maintain themselves. And that, I believe —and people who know a great deal more

I

about it than I do, believe—nothing but Christianity, the love of Christ, can do for them.

4. *"So I returned, and considered all the oppressions that are done under the sun: and behold the tears of such as were oppressed, and they had no comforter; and on the side of their oppressors there was power; but they had no comforter."* [1]

They have no comforter. The present condition of affairs is horrible for the poor; and, rightly viewed, it is equally intolerable for the rich. Even the selfish, those who frankly care for no interest but their own, are tormented by a sense of uneasiness and insecurity. The conventions on which their power stood are shaken; the immemorial rights of property are disputed; they feel that the strength wherein they trusted is passing from them. And the sensitive and enlightened conscience is troubled by nobler questionings. There are some to-day to whom the burden of prosperity so dearly bought grows unendurable; they cannot bear to be the petted children of unequal Fortune, while their brethren are outcast and disinherited. But these finer spirits are not yet able to leaven the whole lump. Most of us think in our hearts that their scruples are quixotic. We are content with the world as we find it. And in proportion to our contentment is our spiritual peril. Now, as in the early days of the Church, "They that will be rich fall into temptations and a snare, and into many foolish and hurtful lusts, which drown men in destruction and

[1] Eccles. iv. 1.

perdition. For the love of money is the root of all evil : which while some covet after, they err from the faith, and pierce themselves through with many sorrows." [1]

Christians are shockingly reckless, and shockingly self-deceived about money. We prefer not to know the history of the cheap merchandise we buy, or the source of the good dividend; and we dream that our ignorance excuses us. We are not traders, we are not directors; their methods are no concern of ours, and there can be no harm in taking what is offered. But, as Dr. Liddon warns us, "There is no such thing as putting personal responsibility into commission, and hoping that God will settle accounts, not with us, but with our commissioners. In this sense no man may deliver his brother, or make agreement to God for him." [2]

Moreover, if we as Christians are blind and reckless in our choice of means for growing rich, we are also amazingly inconsistent in the value we attach to the end. Christ's teaching on this point is plain and unmistakable. He regards wealth as unimportant, except so far as it is dangerous to moral growth. In no case is it a proper object for the serious pursuit of a disciple. "The cares of this world, and the deceitfulness of riches, choke the word, and it becometh unfruitful." "How hardly shall they that have riches enter into the Kingdom of Heaven." "Seek ye first

[1] 1 Tim. vi. 9, 10.
[2] " Sermons on the Old Testament," p. 218.

the Kingdom of God, and His Righteousness, and all
these things shall be added unto you." " Ye cannot
serve God and Mammon." [1]

Our opinion, it would appear, is different—we think
we can serve God and Mammon ; and though we are
inclined on the whole to put Mammon first, we do not
regard that as being in any way inconsistent with a
sufficient and loyal service of God.   In fact, we do not
regard the two things as opposed, but as complementary;
and hence, perhaps, arises the notion, widely held and
simply expressed, that a bishop, of all men, must have
the prestige which attaches to a large income, if he is
to carry on his spiritual work efficiently.   Our reverence
for great wealth would be absurd, if it were not so
mischievous.   It is not hypocrisy, not altogether
snobbery, for it is pathetically genuine and disin-
terested, almost religious in its character.   Men admire
and court a very wealthy person, irrespective of any
advantage they may hope to gain from him : exactly
as we read in the old days men admired a lord.   A
new aristocracy of wealth has taken the place of the
aristocracy of birth and rank, and has even succeeded
to a practical enjoyment of some of its privileges.
And the reason surely is, apart from a natural tendency
to worship what is big and strong and successful, that
these men possess a large quantity of what all men
covet as the chief good of life.   In former times men
desired, above all things, power and consideration, and
they envied and respected those who could command

[1] Matt. xiii. 22 ; Mark x. 23 ; Matt. vi. 33, 24.

them; to-day we desire chiefly comfort verging on luxury. We are rather inclined, too, to make a sort of virtue of our desire and its attainment. One hears it said, with some complacency, that the standard of comfort has risen wonderfully throughout the country in the last fifty years. God knows it might safely rise still more for some hundreds of thousands of our countrymen. But, without reference to Christian principles, it may be questioned, whether making the comfortable classes more comfortable is altogether a gain; and does not rather lead to what R. L. Stevenson calls a fatty degeneration of the whole moral nature. We may fear that the well-to-do classes in this country have already reached a degree of luxury which begins to slacken the will and dull the intelligence. We demand, and get, many things which our grandfathers did without; but are we the better for it? The appliances, which are supposed to make life easier, are becoming a nuisance and a burden to many of us; and, at best, they cost time and thought and money, which could be better bestowed, and so defeat their purpose, adding to the strain of life which they are intended to relieve. The modern craving for comfort is certainly a baser thing than the mediaeval love of magnificence, and it has left its mark on our art and our literature. The men of those days had the genius to build splendidly, and the conviction to destroy without remorse the work of their predecessors. The note of our time is an extraordinarily high level of technical skill with no touch of inspiration. We try to make up for our lack of originality by an almost superstitious reverence for the achievements of the past, which is amply justified by our failure to match them, but is an unerring sign of a decadent civilization.   The failure to produce great works of art, original and characteristic of our own age, is partly due, no doubt, to the fact that many able minds are occupied in making life smoother, instead of making it nobler and more beautiful; but it is also true that soft living does not fit men either to create or to appreciate masterpieces.   It is well if it has not tainted deeper springs of the national character than intellect and sense.

5. So far I have spoken of the secular aspect of this tendency in modern life.   What of its religious aspect? How can we call ourselves Christians, when we are so far from obeying the Apostolic injunction, that having food and raiment, we should be content therewith; when we care so much about money, soft lying, and delicate eating and drinking?   It is something to have been forced to ask ourselves this question—everything, if we are quite honest; for there is in truth but one clear answer.   But in practice we offer many answers, which seem to let us keep what we like so well, and yet satisfy our conscience.

So much has been said and written about social evils, that most of us are a little uneasy about the inequalities of the system in which we happen to occupy a fairly prosperous place. We are shocked, perhaps, by some particularly lurid revelation, and our first instinct is to write a cheque for as much as we can conveniently spare, or even a little more. We may be so deeply impressed that we resolve to subscribe regularly to some charitable object which we understand is excellent; and feel that now we are doing our duty to our neighbour. But it will not serve. This is not Charity, it is ransom—the blackmail which our sins levy on our desire to feel virtuous. It is as bad as giving a shilling to a tramp because we are a little afraid of him, or tired of listening to his whine. However, we are getting educated past that stage. We have learned that it is wicked to give a shilling to a tramp, because it does not help him, but keeps him down, by encouraging him to continue in ruffianism and lying, instead of taking to honest work. That is true, but it is only a half truth. We cannot let people starve while we take a broad and comprehensive view of their cases. What we have to do is to keep the tramp alive till we find out why he is a tramp, and whether he can be cured; and more hopefully inquire how we can prevent his children and other children from becoming tramps. And here, too, we cannot wholly delegate our responsibility, or put it into commission. Charity Organization is a necessary thing and an admirable thing; but it is not infallible, and is sometimes cruel in its working; and, like all things official, is apt to grow tyrannous, if it is not well looked after by lay people. It is therefore our duty to get knowledge for ourselves, and to act on it with sense and prudence, but without compromise.

We are tempted to try a *via media*. We object to almsgiving, and rightly, in so far as the relief it gives is only temporary, and its results, if we do no more than give alms, permanently mischievous. But we have not the courage and sincerity to surrender and abolish what makes almsgiving a necessity and a curse. The reason why we dare not obey literally our Lord's command to give, is that we let our duty to our neighbour begin and end with the gift. We do not face the moral law, which gives virtue to the act. When Christ restored power to the limbs of the paralyzed man, He was not content with the gift of physical health, but gave him guidance and motive to use his new strength rightly. "Behold thou art made whole. Sin no more, lest a worse thing come unto thee."[1]

We have no right for their sake, or for our own, to preach contentment to the poor, or bribe them into acquiescence, until we have given them the elementary justice of an equal opportunity of living the life which God intended for them.

"The principle of justice," says a great preacher who has often pleaded for righteousness from this place, "is one which is not approximately realized in what we call Christian society at present. It is comparatively few men who have a real opportunity of work and remuneration according to their faculties, of spiritual knowledge, of legitimate education, physical and moral."[2]

[1] John v. 14.
[2] Dr. Gore, "The Social Doctrine of the Sermon on the Mount," p. 22.

Until that is secured, until the principle of justice is acknowledged and acted on, all philanthropic effort which teaches contentment, which aims chiefly at the maintenance of the established Social Order, and has not for its purpose a permanent moral improvement, is a wrong to the poor, and a specious anodyne for the consciences of the rich. It is such Philanthropy as this which our Lord pictures as sending men with fatal self-confidence to face the Judgment. "Many will say unto me in that day, Lord, Lord, have we not prophesied in Thy Name, and in Thy Name cast out devils, and in Thy Name done many wonderful works? And then will I profess unto them, I never knew you : depart from Me, ye that work iniquity." [1]

[1] Matt. vii. 22, 23.

LECTURE VI

ANARCHY NOT THE CURE

Φανερὸν ὅτι τῶν φύσει ἡ πόλις ἐστί, καὶ ὅτι ἄνθρωπος φύσει πολιτικὸν ζῷον, καὶ ὁ ἄπολις διὰ φύσιν καὶ οὐ διὰ τύχην ἤτοι φαῦλός ἐστιν ἢ κρείττων ἢ ἄνθρωπος.—ARISTOTLE.

LECTURE VI

ANARCHY NOT THE CURE

"And He saith unto them, Whose is this image and super-scription? They say unto Him, Caesar's. Then saith He unto them, Render therefore unto Caesar the things which are Caesar's; and unto God the things that are God's."—MATT. xxii. 20, 21.

1. THE hope and purpose of Liberal Theology have been, and are more than ever to-day, to make Christianity a possible Religion for the intelligent man of the world. It makes its appeal to common sense by submitting the dogmatic and historical tenets of the Churches without reserve to the tests of critical investigation; and ultimately by presenting Christianity not as a Creed, but as a Life, and faith as the result, not of an intellectual surrender which is felt to be repugnant to sincerity, but of the normal intellectual processes which apply in the sphere of practice and secular knowledge. In the first stage of its endeavour it has been to a great extent successful. Whatever may be our opinion of Liberal Theology, we must at least admit that its methods and results have compelled the educated intelligence of Europe to reconsider most seriously the truth and importance of that which, seventy years ago, it was preparing to dismiss as

unworthy of consideration.   But in its further purpose,
of facilitating the wide acceptance of Christianity, it
has largely and unexpectedly failed.   In clearing away,
rightly or wrongly, the intellectual difficulties, it has
brought men face to face with the real and fundamental
contradiction between Christianity and the world, which
is the Ethical.   The average honest man does not find
things made easier for him at all; he heartily wishes
himself back in the quiet times when Christianity
meant going to church and asking no questions, instead
of obedience to principles entirely opposed to those
which he sees governing the thoughts and actions of
the society in which he is an active member.   This
contradiction presents an insurmountable obstacle to
very many whom intellectual difficulties would not
have much disturbed.   Sensible men commonly allow
themselves to be guided by authority in matters beyond
the range of their personal knowledge and experience;
but in the practical world they feel that they are
qualified and obliged to judge.   And the result is that
they decline to make public profession of a creed which
they see no prospect, and indeed have no intention of
carrying out in their lives.   Their conclusion may
not be right, but it is quite intelligible and logical.
They will not allow their instinctive honesty to be
sophisticated by arguments which interpret the duty
of obeying the spirit, and not the letter, of Christ's
precepts as a justification for not obeying them at all;
and which find in the dominant ethic of each succeeding age a legitimate development of the principles of

Christianity.   But while we regret the loss of such men
to the Church, we must acknowledge that we are deeply
indebted to their sincerity for defining the issue so
sharply, and thrusting the question upon Christians
in a form which forbids either delay or ambiguity in
answering.   They express, in the most unmistakable
manner, their conviction that the man of business and
the man of politics have nothing to do with Christianity under present conditions.   Is the converse true?
Can the Christian under present conditions have anything to do with business and politics?   If the social
order is so radically corrupt that it is the mere expression
of the spirit of selfishness which is the antithesis of
the Christian spirit, can we accept the responsibility
of helping to maintain it, or offer it anything but that
passive submission which is the most powerful solvent
of institutions?   Is the duty of the Christian and the
remedy for the evils of the world to be found in
Anarchy?

Anarchy is an ugly word; it is associated in our
minds with aimless, indiscriminate murders; but for
the present let us separate it from its accidents,
and take it in its plain meaning—a dislike for all
government of man by man, a disbelief in all external
coercion as a means for good.   The spirit of it is
already at work in more subtle and effective ways
than insensate violence.   We are attracted or shocked
by it in the works of certain modern writers, where
it takes the form of a blank and hopeless pessimism,
which despairs of civilization present and future.   The

whole structure of Society is, for them, a monstrous
creation of human folly and wickedness, rendered only
more abominable and more dangerous by the superstition that it benefits and protects its victims.   Law
is chicanery and cruelty organized, tormenting and
slaying with sanctimonious formalities.   Custom is
the dead hand of bygone foolishness and insincerity,
keeping its grasp on new generations, which themselves
do not lack a plentiful supply of these vices.   Public
opinion is the clamour of fools, cajoled and excited
by rogues for their own ends.   Nor is there hope for
the future.   These melancholy philosophers do not
even desire to amend the wrongs they perceive so
clearly.   In their prudence they would rather keep
the ills they have than fly to others that they know
not of.   They hold that revolution is a chimaera, a
change to some new false and cruel system.   In their
eyes the Tyrant and the Reformer, the Criminal and
the Saint, are equally tragic and absurd figures.   They
only ask to be let alone, and console themselves with
the thought that Government and other organized
interferences with the individual are not as strong
and as infallible as their admirers imagine.

Now I think I need not labour an argument to
prove that such anarchy as this can have nothing in
common with Christian thought.   Any pessimism must
be as the poles removed from Christianity, which is
nothing if it is not a Hope.   But there is another kind
of Anarchy, far more cheerful and practical, with which
we are familiar.   It does not sit in the study and distil

its despair into well-balanced periods ; it goes abroad upon the streets to enjoy itself. It thinks well of the world and its prospects, and is instinct with a heady optimism, the child rather of impulse than experience. True, it has its quarrels, too, with law and custom and public opinion : finds convention an irksome garment ; but it believes that a healthy and robust nature can dispense with these old catchwords, and do very well for itself and for Society. Its simple philosophy is summed up in the maxim, " Love your neighbour, and do what you like yourself."

The words give us pause, for indeed these precepts of a genial self-indulgence sound curiously like a summary of the teaching of the Sermon on the Mount. The difference lies in the emphasis ; but it is a world-wide difference. If the two clauses are enunciated as parallel and of equal authority, there is a proba-bility, amounting to a certainty, that the second will encroach upon the first till it has ousted it wherever the two seem to conflict ; or self-love, grown tyrannous and diseased, will infect love for one's neighbour,

> " like a cankered ear,
> Blasting his wholesome brother,"

till love itself is turned to something more foul and deadly than hatred. The end of this philosophy of conduct is seen in ruined and wasted lives, spreading ruin and waste around them, and themselves tormented in an *Inferno* of shattered hopes and satisfied desires.

Christ gives us His counsel in the same words, but

K

He makes the second clause, the permission, dependent and conditional on the fulfilment of the first, the command. It is only when we have fully learned to love our neighbour as ourselves, with all the wisdom it implies, that we can safely do what we like ourselves. That is the perfect law of liberty, of anarchy if you will, but the glorious and innocent anarchy which is the Kingdom of God. And the subordination is not possible without Christ. Even so, even for Christians, it is not a present fact, but a still distant end towards which we are working, and let us say it with all reverence, He is working in us. We cannot pretend that His Kingdom has come in that sense. We may be truly heirs of the Kingdom, but " The heir, so long as he is a child, differeth nothing from a servant, though he be lord of all ; but is under tutors and governors until the time appointed of the father." [1]

A thousand years see the rise and fall of many generations, yet they are but a short period in the history of the Race ; and on the most flattering estimate of progress the most we can claim for Humanity in Science and Morals is that it is emerging from a troublesome childhood into a somewhat petulant youth. Discipline may be changed and modified to suit with growth, but it cannot safely be relaxed. We still need the help and guidance of external coercion, because the rules and limitations which seem to hamper free achievement are really what make any achievement possible for most of us. It is easier to make

[1] Gal. iv. 1, 2.

a passable sonnet than to write good rhythmical prose,
because the rules of the Sonnet are definite and un-
yielding. A stern and narrow discipline best moulds
and tempers our intellectual and artistic faculties for
their highest activity; and the like is true of our
spiritual faculties. We cannot afford to allow anarchy
in ourselves or others, if for no other reason, because
it asks too much of human nature. It assumes that
men are naturally kind, and wise, and loyal, whereas
all experience goes to show that they are the reverse;
and the reformer who acts on the belief that men are,
to start with, all that he would have them to be,
prepares for himself disappointment.

The opinion that the unchecked and unguided
impulses of humanity would not tend to right action,
is not based solely on a belief on the Christian doctrine
of Original Sin, but is strongly confirmed by the
teachings of Science. Evolution in its earliest stages
may be regarded as the result of the free interaction
of natural forces; but from another point of view,
it is not less truly the result of interference with these
forces. The differentiated organism justifies itself by
defeating the natural law which destroys its more
conservative brethren. And as soon as conscious intelligence comes into play, this interference appears as the
determining factor in all higher progress. All cultiva-
tion of plants and animals, with a view to what we
consider valuable qualities, is an unending conflict with
the natural tendency of reversion to type. The culti-
vated fruit tree is not, and never could be, the result of

uninterrupted and unaided development; its excellence is the work of man's hand, and it depends on man for protection. Unaided it cannot stand against its uncultivated kindred; for nature loves her wildings, and the lower forms are the more reproductive. So simple and natural a thing as a grass lawn must be jealously guarded and disciplined if it is to keep its virtue of uniform colour and texture. The sluggard in Dr. Watts's poem left his garden to the free play of natural forces, and we read that the wild briar, the thorn, and the thistle rose highest in that vegetable commonwealth. We cannot tolerate the struggle for life in our gardens; much less shall we endure it, if we are wise, in our state, or in our soul.

I observe that, in this general discussion of anarchy, I may be accused of resorting to a common device of the preacher, setting up an imaginary opponent conveniently accoutred for my attack, and arguing against a position which no one really holds. In secular government and society, I admit, the adoption of anarchic principles is not seriously contemplated by any one who need be considered; the ruling tendency is rather the other way. But in Religion there is a marked movement towards extreme individualism, which is anarchic in its exaggerated dislike of Churches, and of all external aids to a devout life and right conduct, and in a higher estimate of the spiritual capacities of the individual than is warranted by experience.

2. However, it is time to return to the more particular question of the right attitude of the Christian,

not to an ideal Society, but to Society as it actually
exists; and his relation to the present form of these
religious societies which we call the Churches.

Let us, then, first consider the secular side, political,
social, and commercial life as we see it about us, from
day to day. After what I have said in my last Lecture,
it would be impossible for me to maintain that the
Christian is at liberty to adopt its principles and practices
without reserve. There are plainly certain classes of
business which he must not touch at all, either directly
as a principal, or indirectly as a shareholder; and in
other enterprises, though the end is lawful, methods
are commonly employed such as the Christian is forbidden to profit by, or to allow, if he can prevent
them. In these matters every man must be guided
by his conscience, with due consideration for the weaker
brother. The danger hitherto is rather on the side
of laxity than of puritanism. So in national and
municipal politics the Christian is clearly precluded
from using, to secure his ends, many weapons both
popular and effective. He must abstain from all
violence and undue influence. He must not abuse
or misrepresent his opponent's proposals, or his personal
character. Furthermore, cases might arise in which
it would be his duty to resist an unjust law even
to the spoiling of his goods; but he is bound to be
very certain that his motive in such resistance *is*
principle, and not merely dislike of a particular enact-
ment; and it is difficult in a free country, with
representative institutions, to imagine circumstances

which justify a course of action so extreme and
anarchic.

However, the definitely forbidden ground is small
compared with the wide extent of neutral territory,
in which also we must be governed by our Lord's
precept and example. It would be idle to look for
exact guidance in details from His life, or from the
practice of the early Church ; for the conditions have
entirely changed. Jesus was, according to the Flesh,
a Syrian peasant under the early Empire ; and He
accepted fully the limitations of the life He had chosen.
He did not use political power, because He did not
possess it. The first Christians, regarded officially as
a sect of the Jews, were equally powerless on that
side. They had before them very many years of
obscure and patient work, leavening the mass of the
World through the individual conscience, before they
were in a position to employ the machinery of State, or
even public opinion beyond a narrow and despised circle.

Our circumstances are strikingly different. Whether
we like it or not, we have political power, and the
responsibility which power carries with it ; and we
have, as Christians, the further responsibility of pos-
sessing what is still regarded, and increasingly regarded,
as the highest ethical standard. The conditions are so
completely altered that here, if anywhere, we are
obliged to obey Christ's teaching in the spirit, and
not in the letter. I shall therefore not think it
necessary to dwell upon the precise attitude of our
Lord, or of His immediate followers towards the Roman

or Jewish Government of their day ; for I think the
more useful course is to acknowledge frankly that He
regarded social and political institutions as indifferent,
ἀδιάφορα; and to consider exactly what He meant by
ἀδιάφορον.

The study of Church History shows that in spite
of repeated and explicit repudiations of dualistic
theories, Christian thought has steadily tended to a
Manichaean view of ἀδιάφορα, including the material
Universe, as somehow evil, or at any rate not belonging
to God. This view leads to two very opposite conclusions in practice, the puritan and the antinomian.
The second, which argues that the believer can safely
use or abuse all things indifferent as he pleases, without
injury or stain to the higher part of his being, has
emerged from time to time in Christian communities
with startling results; but it is generally rejected by
the common sense and common morality of mankind.
The puritan conclusion, " Touch not, taste not, handle
not," has laid and keeps a firm grip on serious minds
and tender consciences.   Abstinence is a valuable
discipline, and would probably be best for us in more
things than we care to admit; but we must bear in
mind that the ascetic ideal is not the highest, nor is it
Christ's. The Son of Man came eating and drinking,
to show us that man's body and its pleasures belong to
God, and that a natural and temperate enjoyment of
them is part of the service we owe to God.   Much
more, then, does He require of men the full use of their
powers of mind, and of their distinctive power of

concerted and continuous action for the common good. Christ's rule for us in social and political matters may best be gathered from such passages as the Parable of the Talents, where He uses, to enforce His teaching, the figure of the other great ἀδιάφορον, Money.   The lesson is made the more striking when we consider that the servants who are praised and rewarded not only used the talent entrusted to them, but risked something in its profitable employment.   They are commended for courage and energy, as well as for industry.   It is to be observed that we do not find in the canonical versions of the story the profligate servant of the Gospel of the Hebrews, who wasted his Lord's money in riotous living.   It is the pattern of negative virtues, the scrupulous and careful servant, who wrapped his talent in a napkin and kept it quite safe, that is punished for being wicked and slothful.   The apocryphal addition gives a satisfactory literary balance to the story, but it spoils the moral.   The type that our Lord censures in this Parable is not the violent and reckless criminal, but the character which is languid and indifferent in using any faculty it possesses, political power as much as another.   The citizen who fails to exercise his rights, either from scruple or from mere idleness, is a more dangerous anarchist than the man of the dagger and the bomb.   He wrongs himself by leaving his opinion unrepresented ; he wrongs the State by refusing a factor in the result on which its counsels depend ; and he also wrongs his Religion, when he declines to support the cause of justice by

obvious and legitimate means, and so encourages the
idea that Religion has no place in practical affairs.   It
is a plain duty for the Christian to study questions
of imperial and local policy, and to employ all lawful
means, influence as well as vote, to secure their right
settlement.   On the other hand, he will not be content
with securing good legislation, or any other external
machinery for improvement; he will not ascribe to
Acts of Parliament any magical power to change the
thoughts of men's hearts; for he will understand that
they are only important as the record of thought;
it is the spirit, not the institution, that counts.
Accordingly, he will not be a fanatical believer in
the virtue of any particular form of government.   The
tide sets just now in the direction of Democracy.   We
are all, and, I think, not wrongly, inclined to see
in it the proper and congenial environment for the
working of the Spirit of Christ.   But there is no
reason in the nature of things, why an absolute
monarchy, or an oligarchy, should not be administered
on Christian principles.   Christianity, with all its
failures, has made so deep an impression, that all
forms of Government claim a sort of divine right,
maintaining, in theory at least, that their purpose, and
the reason of their being, is to cherish and enforce
righteousness; so that any one of them, if it could
be kept to the level of its professed standard, might be,
under whatever name, a Christian Government.

Meanwhile, we in England have free and representative institutions, under which we are called upon to

choose our leaders, and to give our judgment on great measures and small. It is a form of government in which most responsibility rests on the individual citizen, and certainly not among the least favourable for the development of the spirit of Christianity. And in truth we may venture to say that our legislation is increasingly Christian in spirit; it is growing more just, more merciful, more considerate towards the weak and the suffering and the sinful. It is our business to see that this progress shall be steady and uninterrupted. Laws, as I have said, are significant only as the record of thought; and it is the popular will alone that can enforce them when they are enacted. Public opinion is stronger than Law. Now Christian opinion is too often silent, or speaks with a weak and uncertain voice, because Christians are divided, and are much occupied with their differences; or, again, because they are reticent and afraid to declare themselves openly; or because they think their Religion is concerned with their own personal salvation, and not with the material and moral welfare of all men. We hesitate and compromise because we lack faith, and dare not know our own strength by putting it to the test; and therefore the world goes forward without us and the Christianity we represent, though not altogether, as we must believe, without God. But if we count it our duty to help in doing God's work, and desire the politics and the business of our country to be honest and wholesome, we must not let them alone while we try to save our own souls; we must create a strong, united, articulate

Christian opinion, whose authority is based on the example of Christian lives.

3. There remains, however, the important and highly controversial question of the Church — the question whether it is necessary or expedient for the maintenance of true Religion to have a Society which interprets Divine Truth authoritatively in Creeds, prescribes ritual and ceremony for public worship, and exercises discipline; a Society, therefore, which is exclusive, in the sense that it refuses to recognize as members those who will not accept its beliefs or obey its rules. This is a question which it is difficult to approach without prejudice on one side or the other. I do not mean for opponents of Christianity only, but for earnest and sincere Christians of different schools of thought and different temperaments. Some Christians, influenced partly by early training and association, but also convinced by actual spiritual experience, regard the Church, both in its doctrinal and its ceremonial aspects, as the appointed means of Grace, which has brought them to a knowledge of God. For others, the Church is an imposture, or at best a compromise with the spirit of the World; in their judgment Ecclesiasticism, Sacerdotalism, is the enemy which has withheld or depraved the Truth as it is in Jesus almost from the first. Men, they say, in all ages have come to Christ and been saved by Him, not through the Church, but in spite of the Church.

Confronted with this astonishing conflict of opinion, the Christian naturally appeals to the authority of the Master. But when we inquire whether Jesus contemplated the founding of what we mean by a Christian Church, we must honestly admit that there is nothing to prove it in His extant discourses; nor are we called upon to believe that after His resurrection He revealed to His apostles, in discourses which have not been handed down to us, the details of the organization by which the Gospel was to be spread and maintained in the world. He appears to have been content with the Jewish Church, in which He was born, as a framework for Spiritual Religion. The author of the conception of the Church, as we know it, was, humanly speaking, not Jesus but Paul. Yet to admit this does not surrender the Church's claim to be a divine ordinance, for St. Paul was guided, as we hope to be guided, by the promised Spirit of Truth. He was not merely self-confident and deluded, when he thought he had the Mind of Christ. It was his task to obey the Lord's command in carrying His Gospel to the Gentiles; and in the new conditions he saw that the forms of Judaism, which might lead a sincere Jew straight to the Kingdom, were a snare and a hindrance to the Gentile convert; but he found also, what all Evangelists find, whether among the untried heathen or the lapsed masses who once were Christian, that if you are to call men, if you are to compel them to come in, you must have something for them to come in to, a visible Society where admission is not indeed Salvation, but the first step on the way of Salvation, and a Belief to inspire and guide them.

The germ of the Christian Creeds is to be found in the Words of our Lord. As His ministry drew to its close, and the certainty of His approaching Passion and Death became very vivid in His own Mind, and was repeatedly impressed by Him on the unwilling minds of His disciples, He asks of them as a test of their discipleship that they should confess Him before men, and thereby enrol themselves in the fellowship of those who are ready to suffer with Jesus. " Now that danger approaches, confession is necessary, that the Cause should not perish with the Person." [1] The earlier moral teaching is not abrogated, or replaced by the Confession of Faith; but it is made clear that the way of Salvation is the way of those who confess Jesus. He *is* the Way. The Prayer of Jesus in the seventeenth chapter of St. John gives a new emphasis to the same thought, and throws light upon its inner meaning. " I have given unto them the words which Thou gavest Me : and they have received them, and have known surely that I came out from Thee, and have believed that Thou didst send Me. I pray for them : I pray not for the world, but for them which Thou hast given Me ; for they are Thine. . . . Neither pray I for these alone, but for them also which shall believe on Me through their word." [2]

Doubtless this Belief, this Confession, was asked and given in a very different spirit from the cold intellectual assent which has satisfied the orthodoxy

[1] See P. Wernle, " Beginnings of Christianity," vol. i. pp. 86, 87.
[2] John xvii. 8, 9, 20.

of later ages; and men and women and Churches are nearer to Christ in proportion as they share the first spirit and not the second. Yet the principle is established once for all, by our Lord Himself, that Belief in the Person and Work of Christ is the life of the Christian, the essence of Christianity.

It will, however, very naturally be objected that, if this be granted, it leaves us far short even of the simplest version of the Apostles' Creed. There are many people who say to us, "If that were all—if the message of the Churches were the message of St. Paul to the gaoler at Philippi, 'Believe on the Lord Jesus Christ, and thou shalt be saved, and thine house'— we could receive that; it is the superstructure that puzzles and offends us." And they have right in their complaint. In the deepest and truest sense that *is* all—all that any man needs, all that any Church has a right to ask. And yet to cavil at the Creeds in their extended form, often shows a wilful or ignorant disregard of the history of their making. They are treated as arbitrary and fantastic additions to the simple truths of the Gospel; whereas nearly every article in our Creeds is a protest and a safeguard against arbitrary and fantastic additions. So long as Christianity was taught by eye-witnesses to the simple and ignorant, the simplest and broadest form of words sufficed. But soon learning and intellect claimed their right in the treasure; and imagination ran riot, bewildered by the glories of an authentic Theophany. One heresy after another sprang up; and the Church

was forced to declare and define, and to curb the
extravagances of the human mind with its own
weapons

Now if the Creeds had only this negative function,
they would be indispensable; as the heresies, which
they arose to combat, recur in new aspects and under
new names. But they have also a positive value for
us; they tell us what it concerns us to believe, as
well as what it concerns us to deny; and by happy
chance, or Divine Providence, the making of Creeds
fell upon a time singularly favourable for such attempts.
If we have not in the Nicene Theology the absolute
expression of Divine Truth, we have the projection
of Divine Truth on Greek Philosophy, the strongest
and most delicate fabric ever wrought by human
intelligence and human speech. I know that this fact
appears to some people a sufficient reason in itself for
discarding or restating the Creeds, on the ground that
the forms in which they are expressed are obsolete
and unintelligible. It does not seem so to me. Greek
thought is not dead; it lives as the common element
in the daily thought and speech of all civilized Western
Races; and, therefore, apart from the practical difficulties of restatement, it is the most fitting vehicle
for the common Creed. None the less, if Christianity
is to vindicate its just claims on the intellect, it is
necessary that some of the best minds of every
generation should be steadily and fearlessly at work
on the problems of the Nature of God and His
relation to Man. It is not the philosophical but the

materialistic treatment of Theology that piles up new dogmas.

4. Ceremony and Ritual are so much and so hotly debated, that I should be unwilling to speak of them, and so add my handful to the dust of the conflict, were it not that they are an essential part of the life of an organized Church. Man is a creature of sense as well as intellect; and while the mind properly demands a reasonable account of the ground of faith, the senses, too, cannot safely be refused their share in the worship of the Creator. The recognition of this fact is one among the causes of the notable success of "High" Churches in poor town districts. A beautiful church and beautiful ordered services are an entirely legitimate and truly effective means of stimulating and expressing devotion which will bear fruit in good works. And the historic ritual of a great Church not only brings the worshipper near to God, but joins him in prayer and praise with his brethren in all lands and in all ages; and becomes the symbol of that Communion of Saints which is the essence of Christianity between man and man. Our thoughts naturally turn to the central act of Christian Worship, that Rite which I think all Christians hold to have been ordained by Christ Himself, and which we believe to be necessary, *salva Dei omnipotentia*, for the full Christian life. Such a belief, one might think, would secure for it glad and frequent observance, and lift it above the strife of tongues. We, *praeposteri homines*, relegate it in practice to a second or third place in our worship,

while we debate its accessories with untiring zeal and
acrimony.   Now whatever view we may hold of Sacra-
mental doctrine, we are all agreed in the last resort
that the thing symbolized, the right attitude to God
and Man, is important, and that all externals only
have value as means to this end, and are in themselves
indifferent.   And this, the unimportance of externals,
is the true reason why it is supremely desirable to
have uniformity in ceremonial, that it may be used
almost unconsciously for edification, and not be made
matter of controversy.   Difference leads to discussion,
and discussion tends almost inevitably to give an
intrinsic importance to its subjects.   We have a
melancholy object-lesson in ceremonial disorder and
its results in the Church of England.   One can hardly
be present at a service, especially at the Service, for
the first time in a church where one is a stranger,
without an unwilling curiosity as to the exact shade
of "Ritual" adopted there; and it mars, though it
cannot destroy, the devotional value of our worship.
The Church of England needs many things, but it
needs, perhaps above all, Discipline; for Ceremony
is the atmosphere of Corporate Religion—a condition
of its life.   So long as the air is pure and wholesome
we use it, but we do not think about it.   When we
grow conscious of it, it is a sure proof that there is
something wrong with the atmosphere, or with the
organism that breathes it.

5. I have dwelt perhaps too long upon dogma and
ceremonial, and left myself but little space to consider

L

that most important religious function of a Church—
the constant enunciation of a moral code stricter than
the accepted ethical standards of the day. I think
we are often tempted to misinterpret some of our
Lord's sayings in a sense which is flattering to our
self-esteem; and so to undervalue what we call Legal
Righteousness. Our Lord never undervalues it. He
denounces the Scribes and Pharisees, not for observing
the Law, even in minute details, but for failing to
observe the Law. And in spite of the shortcomings
of their practice, their teaching, as guardians and
exponents of the legal morality, is accounted by Him
worthy of respect. "The Scribes and the Pharisees
sit in Moses' seat: All therefore whatsoever they bid
you observe, that observe and do; but do not ye after
their works: for they say, and do not." [1]

Without going into the larger question, whether
we are justified in disparaging the Law of Moses as
we do, we must acknowledge that it was the high
average morality of the Jews, as compared with other
nations, which made Jewish life and Jewish religion
the fit setting for the ethical teaching of Jesus. And
among them He surely takes the best recognized
standard, not the worst, as the starting-point for what
is still better, the formation of Christian character,
when He says: "Except your righteousness shall
exceed the righteousness of the Scribes and Pharisees,
ye shall in no case enter into the Kingdom of
Heaven." [2]

[1] Matt. xxiii. 2, 3.   [2] Ibid., v. 20.

We should probably maintain that any branch of the Christian Church presents a Rule of Conduct at once more intelligent and more spiritual than the Law ; and still we are inclined to depreciate its specific commands and prohibitions : implying that we have kept all these from our youth up, and are passing now into a higher sphere of morality, where these elementary safeguards are no longer a help or a guide. But are we quite sincere ? Are we perfectly certain that we have exhausted the ethical content even of that extremely modified Christianity which cannot remove mountains, but does tell us broadly that certain things are right, and certain other things wrong ; and that we ought to eschew the evil and choose the good ? Our Lord has a terrible word for people who neglect the old-fashioned rules and sanctions of their religion on the plea that they need something more transcendental to influence them : " If they hear not Moses and the Prophets, neither will they be persuaded, though one rose from the dead." [1]

[1] Luke xvi. 31.

LECTURE VII

CHRISTIANITY A REVOLUTIONARY FORCE

" The will of God, as it is fully and completely contained in
the Sermon on the Mount, is no less entirely distinguished from
the claims of the later Church than from the Jewish Law : and it
ought really to produce an impression of entire novelty among us
at the present day."—PAUL WERNLE.

LECTURE VII

CHRISTIANITY A REVOLUTIONARY FORCE

"Except ye be converted, and become as little children, ye shall not enter into the Kingdom of Heaven."—MATT. xviii. 3.

1. No very subtle casuistry is needed to convince, no very urgent entreaty to persuade the average professing Christian that he has a right and a duty to take his place in the political and economic framework of society; and that he can, if he is reasonably careful, use the existing forms to good ends, without compromising his religious principles. But it is quite another thing to make ourselves realize the complementary duty, and understand that we are bound, in using those forms, to transmute their methods and results to something wholly different from what we have hitherto accepted, under the guidance of a transformed will, and a changed judgment of values. To maintain that Christianity is a revolutionary force is to balance dangerously between paradox and platitude. On the one hand, the phenomena of conversion and the changed life of individuals is so familiar, at least in theory, that, unless they can be presented in some novel and striking form, they have almost ceased to captivate the imagination. And, on the other hand, in the political and social sphere, it

would seem absurd or insincere to speak of Christianity
as an influence which makes for radical reforms. Orthodox Christians are commonly thought old-fashioned;
and the Church is, not quite unjustly, identified in the
public mind with timid conservatism in politics. The
mass of professing Christians themselves regard their
religion as something static rather than dynamic. They
would fain be tarrying all their lives in the Interpreter's
house, instead of tramping the open road with Mr.
Greatheart, through difficulty and peril and extreme
discomfort, but on towards the Heavenly City.

If we examine this singular but not unnatural state
of mind, we shall find, I believe, that it is a great cause
of the Failure which is the subject of these Lectures;
and it has its root in that deep instinct of the human
mind, which allows every human being to regard himself
and his immediate surroundings as exempt from the
operation of general laws which he cheerfully recognizes
when applied to others. We expect Faith to move
mountains and to change the face of the world, when
we will not allow it to change the least of our own
habits and opinions.

Now an instinct is a hard thing to combat; and if
it were seriously argued, instead of being merely taken
for granted, that Christianity is a bland reactionary
influence whose virtue it is to make people content
with themselves as they are, and teach them to look
back instead of forward for the Golden Age, I should
have more confidence in citing evidence to the contrary.
Moreover, that evidence is, as I have said, the merest

commonplace of religious history and experience. Yet, in consideration of the practical disregard of it, you must forgive me if I insist on the fact, that in any age, when Christianity has had a real hold on the lives and consciences of men, neither its disciples nor its enemies have given any encouragement to this comfortable view of it. The words which startled Nicodemus— "Except a man be born again, he cannot see the Kingdom of God"—have had their literal meaning and their fulfilment in every generation ; and in every age those who were chiefly interested in the maintenance of things as they are, have seen Christianity, not as restful and reassuring, but dangerous and subversive.

The Pharisees and Sadducees saw it very clearly ; they saw their political and religious supremacy undermined, their prudent compromises all shaken and discredited ; and they were, not unnaturally, irritated and alarmed. "If we let Him thus alone, all men will believe on Him : and the Romans shall come and take away both our place and nation. And one of them, named Caiaphas, being the high priest that same year, said unto them, Ye know nothing at all, nor consider that it is expedient for us that one man should die for the people, and that the whole nation perish not." [4]

Doubtless the High Priest's words bore, as the Evangelist tells us, a deeper significance than he knew ; but in the first place they show a keen political judgment, a true appreciation of the nature of the force which had arisen to confront him.

[1] John xi. 48–50.

So, too, when the Jews of Thessalonica cried out, "These that have turned the world upside down are come hither also;" when Demetrius, the silversmith, and his fellow - craftsmen raised a riot at Ephesus; they were, no doubt, moved by envy, and by the menace to trade interests, but none the less they were paying an involuntary tribute to the real purpose and meaning of St. Paul's Gospel.

As time went on, and the Church grew, and grew stronger, Imperial Rome itself was forced to see Christianity as a revolutionary force. The true relations of the Roman Government with Christianity are obscured by popular ideas of the cruelty and malignity of persecutors. It is not to the Acts of the Martyrs, but to the letter of Pliny and the rescript of Trajan, that we must go for information, if we want to form a correct judgment of the official attitude. These documents present an interesting picture of the humane and sensible governor, puzzled by an entirely new factor in the problems which he had to handle; brushing aside the absurd and monstrous calumnies which popular ignorance and spite levelled at the Christians; most unwilling to punish them, and yet convinced that their meek obstinacy was somehow a danger to the power which he represented. It is equally interesting to observe that Trajan, while fully alive to the perils of a system of delation, and deter-mined to repress it, felt none the less that the self-convicted Christian must suffer in the interest of the State. And the instinct which led these good and wise men to act in a way which seems to us unpardonable, was a sound one. If the Imperial system was to be maintained, Christianity could not be tolerated. The whole splendid fabric of Roman Government rested on a working belief in the Divine mission of the Emperor, and its continuance was incompatible with a Creed, however harmless and beneficent in other respects, which exalted Jesus of Nazareth, an obscure provincial, above the personified deity of Rome.

So for two centuries more the persecution went on, now fiercer, now more languid; and Christianity flourished in spite of it, and because of it; till the day came when the cold sagacity of Constantine observed that a policy of repression had become impracticable. He eluded the alternative of unconditional surrender by a compromise, and found a useful ally in the power which threatened to destroy him. His dexterous policy admitted his rival to a share of the Purple: by allowing the Church to become Caesar, he secured his own position as Augustus. And so the Faith, which fear and pain had not shaken, was, in some degree, bewitched and corrupted by wealth and dignity. The World, as Bishop Westcott says, got into the Church in the fourth century, and we have never been able to get it out since.

2. And here, I think, we touch again upon one at least of the causes of Failure we are seeking. If I may use a somewhat bold metaphor—which has, if you will think of it, a very high authority—the cunning Spirit of the World takes the ferment which

worked such radical changes in the constitution of
the human soul, and by inoculating Society at large
with a very dilute and attenuated serum, secures
for it a measure of immunity from violent and incon-
venient attacks. The result is only too familiar to
us all. In any nation or class where Christianity is
an inherited habit, or an accepted convention which
every one takes as a matter of course, the normal
religious experience of the individual is a very mild
and manageable form of the fever which consumed
St. Paul and wrung from him the agonized cry,
" Wretched man that I am ; who shall deliver me from
this body of death ? " We find what is called Average
Christianity acting as a protection against enthusiasm,
a positive obstacle to genuine conversion. Happily—
or, I would rather say, by the mercy of God—the
immunity it provides is not complete. I believe that
since Christ came there has been no generation so dull
and selfish, no Church so fallen into superstition and
formalism, but it held some souls that understood, and
faced the teaching of Christ in all its terror and all its
beauty, and made the great venture. And from time
to time prophets have arisen with power to preach
Christ as He is to men, and to compel them to forsake
all and follow Him. Then there has come a great
spiritual awakening ; a copy, though it may be faint
and imperfect, of what happened in Galilee and
Judaea nineteen hundred years ago. Such was the
first coming of the Friars ; such the Protestant Reformation, with all its mistakes ; the Methodist Revival

in the eighteenth century ; the Tractarian movement in the nineteenth.

And observe that in every one of these attempts to realize Christianity we can trace the same stages of progress and reaction which we have noted on a large scale in the history of the first four centuries. There is in each case the long silent preparation, the sudden enthusiasm and success which drives vested interests and established respectabilities from contempt to alarm and open hostility—to axe and faggot in the old days, to frantic abuse and misrepresentation in less forcible times—and when these fail, there is still the subtler policy of compromise. The world adopts whatever is external and non-moral in the new movement, giving it its place in the accepted ceremonial of Religion, as we are told that the Emperors were ready to admit the image of Christ also among the gods of the tolerated Pantheon. And the World too commonly has had its measure of success. It cannot meet the wild, untameable Spirit of Christianity face to face. But it can turn aside its onset by courting its disciples instead of persecuting them ; and by giving them vested interests of their own to guard, it quenches the fierceness of their attack upon its prosperity and peace of mind. And so, again and again in the history of mankind, we see the troubling of the waters die away to a ripple. The children of this world prove wiser in their generation than the children of light—

> " Et minax, quod sic voluere, ponto
> Unda recumbit."

So it seems; but so it is not. The form of each one of these revivals is determined by circumstances, and perishes in the using; but the spirit of them is undying, its force indestructible. Every genuine effort to obey the Mind of Christ, whether it is a great national movement for Righteousness, or the secret prayer of an individual disciple, helps to raise permanently the spiritual level of mankind.

> "For while the tired waves vainly breaking
> Seem here no painful inch to gain,
> Far back, through creeks and inlets making,
> Comes silent flooding in the main."

The moral of all these apparent failures of noble purpose is not despondency nor acquiescence, but unwearied effort; or, if I may borrow the happier language of a wise man, who, if he was not a Christian after our way, had sometimes a very clear vision of God, "The true conclusion is to turn our back on apprehensions, and embrace that shining and courageous virtue, Faith. Hope is the boy, a blind, headlong, pleasant fellow; Faith is the grave, experienced, yet smiling man. Hope lives on ignorance: open-eyed Faith is built upon a knowledge of our life, of the tyranny of circumstance, and the frailty of human resolution. Hope looks for unqualified success; but Faith counts certainly on failure, and takes honourable defeat to be a form of victory."[1]

That is the lesson of past failures; and their warning is, first, that we must not look back but forward—must

[1] R. L. Stevenson, "Virginibus Puerisque," p. 41.

find our Christ, not in a remote past, but here and now; for our Master does not belong to one century or another, but all Time and Eternity are His. Except He be in us and we in Him, St. Paul cannot save us, nor St. Francis, nor Luther, nor Wesley, nor Newman. We must, therefore, be on our guard against giving absolute value to the outward forms in which any of them brought the Truth to the men of his own generation, lest we be tempted to idolatry, and forget the Spirit which made those forms life-giving. And, second, these failures serve to remind us that Christianity, in its vital manifestations, has been, and has been considered, a revolutionary force. It has sometimes, though not often, appeared to strike directly at the constitution of Government and Society; but in every case it does certainly and immediately question, and even contradict, maxims and principles on which most men conduct their lives without discredit, and without realizing, or at least without admitting, that those principles are wrong or insufficient. For a man's duty to himself—that easy and comprehensive obligation —it substitutes his duty to God and to his neighbour; or, rather, it insists that a man's duty to God and to his neighbour is identical with—*is* his duty to himself. Accordingly, the whole system of checks and prohibitions, which were found necessary to restrain self-love from outrageous manifestations, is merged and summarized in a positive quality of character. "For this, Thou shalt not commit adultery, Thou shalt not kill, Thou shalt not steal, Thou shalt not bear false witness,

Thou shalt not covet; and if there be any other commandment it is briefly comprehended in this saying,
namely, Thou shalt love thy neighbour as thyself.
Love worketh no ill to his neighbour, therefore love
is the fulfilling of the law." [1]

No doubt it has already occurred to some of my
readers that the very phrase I offer as typical of the
distinctive spirit of Christianity is itself quoted, word
for word, from Leviticus,[2] and therefore must be credited
not to the Gospel but to the Law.   But in the context
there the meaning of *neighbour* is sharply limited by
the words which precede: "Thou shalt not avenge
nor bear any grudge *against the children of thy people*,
but thou shalt love thy neighbour as thyself."   Doubtless this precept, with all its limitations, was a great
advance in charity and unselfishness, and indeed remains
to this day for many professing Christians a counsel
of perfection.   But our Lord Himself, in the Sermon
on the Mount, notes its fatal defect as a rule of life,
by adding the complementary permission which men
found implicit in it: "Ye have heard that it hath
been said, Thou shalt love thy neighbour and hate
thine enemy.   But I say unto you, Love your enemies
. . . that ye may be the children of your Father
which is in heaven." [3]

And He shows us that in truth it is a maxim, not
of morality but of self-interest, and practised by those
who make no claim to a high moral standard: "If ye

[1] Rom. xiii. 9, 10.   [2] Lev. xix. 18.
[3] Matt. v. 43, 44, 45.

love them which love you, what reward have ye? do not even the publicans the same?"[1]

The words, it is true, stand written in the law: and He came not to destroy the law but to fulfil; but His fulfilment differs not in degree only, but in principle, from all that went before. And it is this fulfilment, this interpretation, which is binding upon us. In the old theory of life every soul, however enlightened and civilized, is in the last resort an Ishmael, standing for itself against the powers of Nature, against all other human souls, and even in a sense against God, in so far as it holds itself outside and apart from Him; now making Him, as even the devout Jews were so ready to do, a partisan in its quarrels; now setting up its will against His will in the pursuance of selfish ends. In the new theory this antagonism, this distinction, vanishes; each soul is a member of Christ, and cannot prosper or suffer to itself alone.

3. This change in the point of view, whether it be sudden or gradual, is what we mean by Conversion. And, as I have said above, and at the risk of being tedious will repeat, we all of us are perfectly ready to admit that this change has taken place in countless human beings. We acknowledge that it is a radical change, not only affecting external actions, but re-creating the inmost being, and transfiguring the whole aspect of Life. We allow that it is a necessary change, that without it a man cannot come into the right relation with God and his fellow-men. But by that singular

[1] Matt. v. 46.

M

gift of abstraction which enables each of us to contemplate his own case as unique and apart, we do not apply these truths to ourselves, while we accept them as being of universal and undoubted application to all ages, nations, and classes but our own.

For instance, we deplore with entire candour the frigid self-approval of the Pharisee, the comfortable formalism of the Sadducee; we understand that it was impossible for these men, with their conception of Righteousness, to become disciples of Jesus of Nazareth, to be anything but His enemies and traducers. We feel, quite sincerely, that even for so good a man as Nicodemus it is true that he could not see the Kingdom of God without passing through a change so vital that it must be called a new birth. And it is even so with another type of accepted virtue which we find in the centurion Cornelius—a character instinct with the old Roman spirit of order and discipline—the fine flower of paganism even now reaching forward to a belief in the one true God, yet lacking something to make it complete. And over against the respectabilities of that age are its abjects—the publican, the harlot, the slave, the jailer, with their conventions of sordid gain, and petty tyranny, and sensual pleasure. There could be no sharper contrast, no wider variety. Yet to all these—to the self-righteous Jew, to the Roman soldier, to the parasites and scourges of a corrupt society—we believe that Christ brought the change, the one change, the utter change, that could make them new creatures, and save them from desperate

and hopeless wickedness, from routine, from complacency.
We believe, and we admire ; and remain, on the whole,
personally as unconcerned as David was while he listened
to Nathan telling his story.

And when we pass from the record of Christianity
in those primitive times to Western Europe in the
Middle Ages, we are equally at our ease.   I have been
reading lately a clever partisan book, written with
the avowed object of exploding what the author sup-
poses to be a prevalent delusion, the Myth of the
so-called Age of Faith.[1]   With much that is interesting
he brings together a great deal of sordid and shocking
detail as to the lives and manners of the people of
that time.   I do not know that the book has anything
to tell us that is really new to students of history ;
but it does serve to emphasize the tremendous contrast ;
and shows us how quickly and vigorously the world
revolted against the practical Christianity of St. Francis
of Assisi's teaching, as soon as it was rid of the charm
of his personality.   The moral the writer draws is that
the ascetic sanctity at which the first Franciscans aimed
was merely a reaction from the monstrous cruelty
and sensuality of the times, and itself, in fact, no less
monstrous and unreasonable.   The moral the average
Christian reader of the twentieth century will be inclined
to draw is that the great saints and great sinners of
the thirteenth have equally little bearing on the moral
and religious problems of his own time and his own
soul.   But suppose that the true moral were that the

[1] G. G. Coulton, " St. Francis to Dante."

Saints were right after all, and that their ideal is as far removed from ours as it was from that of Machiavelli, and worse men than Machiavelli.[1]

But, indeed, we manage to bring the case much nearer to our own time and place without letting it touch ourselves. We realize so fully the spiritual deadness and dulness of England under the Georges, that we are sometimes inclined to exaggerate it. And passing at once to the present, let me cite briefly two salient instances of the change which Christianity still has the power to work in human life and character. And I would ask you to observe that we do not question the fitness of the method or the value of the result; we are even ready to assist, with a greater or less degree of enthusiasm, these or similar efforts to extend the blessings of Christianity to other people. And yet we manage to regard them all the time as if they applied to beings of another genus, another world, than our own; proceeding, I fear, tacitly on the presumption that we are adequately Christian already—just persons who need no repentance.

I take, then, two examples, of which I happen to know something in detail. Sixty years ago the Melanesian Mission found the islanders of that great Archipelago typical heathen savages. I will say nothing of many ugly aspects of savage life, which we are apt to overlook, while we dwell rather on what

[1] I take Machiavelli, though he does not belong to the thirteenth century, as the sincere exponent of the non-Christian theory of life in mediaeval Italy.

we conceive to be its romantic and picturesque sides.
I will speak only of two dominant influences, which
darkened their whole existence, each in turn giving
fresh strength to the other—Hatred and Fear.   Every
island, every clan, every village, lived in perpetual
war with its neighbour.   Within the compass of one
small island there would be two or three tribes speaking different tongues, and holding no intercourse except
the intercourse of rapine and murder.   And what stood
to them in the place of religion was abject fear—fear
of malignant spirits, fear of witchcraft.   The reef
where they fished was haunted by other ghostly fishers
whose quarry was men's lives; the forest was full of
demons waiting to catch the unwary traveller; the
night was possessed with the horror of great darkness.
And ever about their path and about their bed was
the fear of magic that could kill them in torments,
and does still kill the heathen islanders.   Under the
shadow of their hideous legends and fancies, strong
men suffered the miseries of a nervous child with a
cruel and superstitious nurse.   From these two plagues
Christianity has delivered them; it has taught them
that all men are brethren, and saved them from the
curse of unreasoning hatred; it has lifted the cloud
of fear from their lives—the fear of darkness, the
fear of magic, and the panic cruelty that always goes
with that fear.   And it would be perversely false to
say that this has come to them by mere contact with
European civilization, when we remember what the
coming of the white man *without religion* has meant

to the native races of the Pacific. Surely it is little wonder that the cry for Christian teachers goes up from all the islands. It is a great wonder, and a great reproach to the Church of England if that cry goes up unanswered.

But if we are called to be evangelists, we must not forget that we are first called to be disciples. While we have to teach the heathen, we have also to learn from him. And in foreign Mission work, the very greatness of the outward change which accompanies conversion may obscure the lesson, and help us still to regard it as something remote from ourselves and our needs. So my other example is chosen from much nearer home, among men and women whose Christianity does not manifestly change the outward circumstances of their lives, but leaves them working, and suffering, and maybe starving, as they were before, and yet makes the whole world of time and eternity a different thing for them. When I speak of the miracle of Christianity among the poor in East and South London, I desire to guard myself most carefully from slipping into a patronizing tone of superiority. If we are to do anything for them, we must realize that the truth is, and the difficulty is, that in some things they are better than the classes who have yet the duty of guiding them and enlightening them. I believe, as indeed we are bound to believe, if we read our New Testament, that the essential virtues of Christianity are not less, but more common, among the poor than among ourselves, and I believe that they are found

too in those who are guided by no conscious religious
belief. It is good that we should understand this,
for it both gives us hope and makes us humble. But
the knowledge does not blind us to the existence of
sin and misery, of brutality and self-indulgence ; and
on the other hand, of hopeless unhappiness and dull or
reckless despair, not to be cured but by Faith in Jesus
Christ. Those who have worked among the poor bear
witness that it does cure them. They tell us of coarse
and wicked lives purified, of selfish lives ennobled,
and of suffering and want and death faced, not with
stoical resignation, but with serene happiness. The
Spirit of Christ does, here to-day, work the utter
change from sin to holiness, from bitter, unsatisfied
revolt to peace and joy ; it does give a meaning and
a glory to life which cannot be touched by weariness
or pain or poverty.

And last, we are ready to admit it for individuals
of our own class. When Religion has a real hold on
a man, when he is converted, he is literally a different
man from what he was before—different from those
to whom the awakening has not come. The outward
change may not be great ; he still shares keenly in
the common life of work and amusement ; but his
outlook, his purpose, and the value he puts on things,
are quite changed. Not once or twice only, but many
times in my life as a schoolmaster and a college tutor, I
have seen the change come : I have seen boys and men
refuse the pleasant path which lay open before them,
and choose a life of drudgery and narrow means, that

offered little hope of men's praise, only the reward of duty done. Or they might make no outward change at all, and follow to the end the career they had chosen, as soldier, lawyer, man of business, or what it might chance to be, but with a new meaning for success, a new sense of their duty to God, to their neighbour, and to themselves. And I am as sure as that I stand here, that it was Christ who worked that change, and that He can work the like radical change in all men— if we will. But it is desperately hard for any one of us to make the effort of will which is necessary for effective Belief. We can see the truth for every creature but ourselves; we can see that their natural instincts and tolerated practice are deplorably at variance with the Ideal which is to bring Salvation to the world ; that their character needs a revolutionary change, a new motive, a new outlook. And we cannot deny that they are men of like passions with ourselves. And yet we are sure that our ways, our ideas and opinions, our conventions and habits, must be somehow consistent with Christianity. They are so comfortable, so hallowed by usage, and, as we are convinced in spite of apparent discrepancies, so essentially moral—in a word, so clearly right and reasonable—that any doctrine which conflicts with them must be questionable, if not heretical.

But, in fact, every unconverted life is equally remote from the spirit of Christianity ; if I may use an old-fashioned phrase, equally displeasing to God.

4. I believe that we are on the verge, if indeed we

are not unawares in the midst, of one more great
Religious Movement, perhaps the greatest the world
has known. The principle which inspires it comes,
on the intellectual side, from our old enemy and helper
Science in the doctrine of the Unity of all Life and
Force; on the social side, it appears in the reaction
against that exaggerated individualism which, like
Cain of old, denies corporate responsibility : its religious
aspect is a quickened belief in the brotherhood of all
men in Christ. I have called it a religious movement,
and it is essentially religious ; but if accredited religions will have nothing to do with it, it will go
on nevertheless, inevitable and irresistible. But if it
is Christianized, if it is fearlessly claimed for Christ
and guided by His Spirit, it will make the world
Christian.

To make the world Christian. The words imply
a revolution so tremendous that the mere naming of
it moves experience to an incredulous smile, and makes
enthusiasm itself falter. And yet it is the task which
our Lord laid upon His disciples, the task in which
all baptized Christians, lay or cleric, man or woman,
are solemnly pledged to take their part. And that
we may be fit to take our part there is one thing
needful ; if we are to help at all in making the world
Christian, we must first be really Christians ourselves ;
and I fear there is no doubt that for the most of
us, for all except a very few, that means we must
become Christians. We must learn, with pain and
wonder, to look on existence as Christ looked on it.

If we cling to the old values, and are content to rule our lives by the compromises and catchwords of worldly wisdom ; if we are satisfied with ourselves and our standards—then we need conversion : the starved, commonplace spirit of us must suffer a change "into something rich and strange" before we have a right to call ourselves disciples of Jesus Christ, or profess to be forwarding His cause in the world.

"Except ye be converted, and become as little children, ye cannot enter into the Kingdom of Heaven." The familiar verse warns us that we cannot even begin the Christian life unless we are ready to give up much that we prize, much that we have given time and trouble to acquire ; much outwardly in consideration, wealth, and comfort ; much inwardly in pride, indifference, and the timidity which we call prudence.

"Become as little children." If we took the words seriously, they would seem repellent or absurd to people who value themselves chiefly on cautious judgment, business acumen, and a proper sense of their position.

We have all, I suppose, been amused and embarrassed by the way children ignore social distinctions, and actually take it for granted that we stand in the ordinary human relation to our servants and their class. Children soon grow wiser, and learn that there are bounds which they may not pass over, and that a breach of the convention is confusing and unwelcome to their humble friends. Of course the question is not a simple one ; it is infinitely difficult, and complicated by the fact that the class feeling is just as strong among the poor as among the rich, and instinctively resentful and suspicious of any attempt to cross the border. But it remains that class distinctions, which do not seem to grow fainter with the advance of political democracy, are the great barrier to Christian work, for they seem to make impossible the sympathy and open speaking which are the condition of Spiritual influence.

The very existence of such a dilemma proves how profound a revolution in human thought and feeling is needed before Society can be brought into accord with Christian principles. But it proves also that this revolution must be in its origin not outward, brought about by legislation or by violence, but inward and spiritual, essentially the reform of character, not of institutions. Doubtless with the reform of character institutions also would change, but in what direction and with what effect in detail it is not easy nor very useful to conjecture. I have had occasion in these Lectures to compare and contrast the spirit of Christianity with the ethics of many forms of polity realized or imagined ; and looking back over what I have said, I find that my conclusions have been mainly negative. We can tell in many points what a really Christian Society would not be like ; what it would be like we cannot tell with certainty, for want of experience. We have seen, I think, that it would not be realized in any actual or imaginary State of Nature, or Tolstoian Anarchy, which ascribes to human nature, untaught

and undisciplined, a virtue which is denied it alike by
experience and by the Christian doctrine of Sin. Still
less perhaps can it be identified with the Social System
now generally existing, with its maxims of expediency
and compromise, its toleration of misery and oppression
in some classes as the basis of ease and culture in
others, and its acceptance of selfishness as the only
and even as the right motive of human action. While
men are men and not angels, they must have some
social order and discipline to help and support their
weakness ; on the other hand, the existing order does
not seem to fulfil the office of constraining, or even
of enabling us to bear one another's burdens. Some
change is needed. But all the more we must be on
our guard against rashly identifying the spirit of
Christianity with any of the definite schemes of
political and social reform hitherto offered to us. It
is easy to distinguish it from the pedantic individualism
which has resulted in the horrors of unrestrained competition and monopoly. And indeed for the moment
such thorough-going individualism is discredited. We
are more tempted to turn to the rising sun of Socialism,
a name of terror or of promise as it may be, but to-day
indifferent to no one. And we do well to turn to it,
and study it long and earnestly, for there is much
in it that comes from Christ and makes for His cause.
Its ideals are truly and profoundly Christian. But
Socialism, as we know it, has not always kept its policy
true to its ideals. It has been tempted to make—nay,
it has already made—its appeal to selfishness ; and,

so far, has become a disintegrating instead of an uniting
force.   The true Socialism is one aspect of Christianity,
and cannot exist apart from it; but there is a pressing
danger that in our enthusiasm we may entangle our
Christianity in the details of a programme, and be
content with the effort to make men act unselfishly
in this or that against their wills, instead of training
the unselfish character to blossom into right action.
In truth, all sincere political theories have their place
in the system of the Christian State; it will use them
all—the ideal of kingship, the ideal of aristocracy, the
ideal of personal liberty, the ideal of common responsibility—in due balance and co-ordination; for not one
of them is naturally alien and incapable of being
Christianized.

Christianity as a rule of life is indeed *identical* with
none of them, but its spirit is far more sharply con-
trasted with popular ideas of Religion, ideas so congenial
to the human mind that they reassert themselves from
age to age—the idea that Religion is a separate and
intermittent activity, confined to its own times and
places, claiming at most one part of life, and leaving
the rest to other activities in which it has no share;
and the idea that it is a method of escaping deserved
punishment by the use of prescribed formulas and
ceremonies.   We know that both these superstitions
pass by the name of Christianity.   We know by
humiliating experience how difficult it is to exclude
some tincture of them from our own conception of it.
But real Christianity has nothing in common with

them; it is not accommodating or indulgent; it will not wait upon our leisure, or condone our pleasant vices; but inexorably demands the whole of our being, emotion, will, and intellect, the whole of our life, thought, speech, and action; and thereby unquestionably declares itself a revolutionary force; so revolutionary that it can afford to leave human institutions unaltered for the moment. The outward framework of Government and Society is indifferent, and can be used for good or evil; but no thought of man's heart is indifferent, and it is the sum of men's thoughts alone that gives the Spirit that can inform the frame, and mould it gradually and silently into an instrument for Righteousness.

"The Kingdom of Heaven is like unto leaven, which a woman took, and hid in three measures of meal, till the whole was leavened." [1]

[1] Matt. xiii. 33.

LECTURE VIII

SOME PRACTICAL CONSIDERATIONS

" *Q. What is the duty of man?*

" *A*. To assist his fellows, to develop his own higher self, to strive towards good in every way open to his powers, and generally to seek to know the laws of Nature, and to obey the Will of God; in whose service alone can be found that harmonious exercise of the faculties which is identical with perfect freedom."—OLIVER LODGE.

LECTURE VIII

SOME PRACTICAL CONSIDERATIONS

"Turn Thee again, thou God of Hosts, look down from heaven :
behold and visit this vine; and the place of the vineyard that Thy
right hand hath planted; and the branch that Thou madest so
strong for Thyself."—Ps. lxxx. 14, 15.

ON this Sunday morning I come to the end of my
task and of my opportunity. I hope I have not proved
quite unworthy of that opportunity and of the patient
hearing your kindness has given me Sunday after
Sunday. I trust that I have been enabled to speak
intelligibly some part of the thought that was in me,
for I believe that, however it has been spoiled and
travestied by faulty utterance, it was a thought worth
speaking, not as mine, but as a message of Christ.
But to-day, as I stand here for the last time as Bampton
Lecturer, my mind cannot help dwelling on the things
that I have left unsaid, the things that I have said
amiss; and I know that it is too late for me now to
fill up much that is lacking; to make the crooked
straight, and the rough places plain. And so the
words I have taken as the text of this last Lecture
are chosen to carry our minds back to the verse which
stood at the head of the first: "When I looked that

N

it should bring forth grapes, wherefore brought it forth wild grapes?"

1. We feel, I think, that it is the Prophet, not the Psalmist, who has drawn the truer meaning for us from this figure of the Vine and the Vineyard of the Lord. If there is failure, it is not because "the wild boar out of the wood doth root it up : and the wild beasts of the field devour it,"[1] not because "her hedge is broken down;" there are only too many hedges. The failure lies in this, that when He looks that we should bring forth grapes, we bring forth wild grapes. Oppression and persecution are not the Reproach of the Gospel, they are its glory. Its shame is the lives of Christians. "By their fruits ye shall know them." And what are the fruits of Christian character as we know it in ourselves? Surely not the bounteous clusters which are the natural fruit of the wholesome, tended, disciplined vine, fruit to make glad the heart of man— but the scanty, wizened, sour bunches of the wild vine, *raris labrusca racemis*, the fruit of self-will and indiscipline that has not known the hand of the Gardener. "Turn Thee again, thou God of Hosts, look down from heaven : behold and visit this vine."

But let us leave the Prophet and the Psalmist, and descend at once from the solemn dignity of Old Testament metaphor to the commonplace realities of our own place and time. We are all agreed, I think, that reform is needed, in social and industrial conditions, in the lives and characters of individuals, and even

---

[1] Ps. lxxx. 13.

possibly in our own character and life. The question is whether a return to the principles of Christ's teaching offers a practical way to that Reform. And this question involves another; namely, whether Christ intended His Church to be universal or to be a limited body of believers saved out of a lost world. If the latter was what He intended, *cadit quaestio;* for on the one hand, in that case, Christianity is not a failure, having continuously fulfilled this purpose since the time of its foundation; and on the other, it has no bearing on the problems of Society. We must admit that this view has been widely held, and that it can be rather cogently supported from Holy Writ; notably by certain passages in St. Paul's Epistles and St. John's Gospel. I am not going to argue the question at length; but I think I am justified in saying that it is based on a confusion between the fact and the ideal, and that the distinction is quite clearly drawn in the New Testament. As a fact, the Christian Church is, and always has been, a body of the elect, chosen out of the world; and this is not *merely* temporary or accidental. The Church preserves itself by separation, and teaches by contrast. But on the other hand, its ideal is to become an universal Society with a common rule of life binding on all men whatever. And I conceive that this Ideal is vitally true and essential, insomuch that Christianity *fails* in proportion as it tends to remain limited and exclusive, and *succeeds* in proportion as it tends to widen its influence over all classes and individuals and all departments of life. An impartial study of the New Testament shows that this Ideal was always present to the minds of the first Christian writers; it is definitely expressed in such passages as the following from St. John and St. Paul: "He is the propitiation for our Sins: and not for ours only, but also for the sins of the whole world."[1] "God our Saviour, who will have all men to be saved and to come to a knowledge of the truth."[2]

2. I do not labour the point, because I think I may take it that there is a consensus among Christians to-day that Christ did mean His Kingdom to be universal, and that the extension of His Kingdom is the way out of many evils which the kingdoms of this World have brought into existence. But there is no such consensus as to the steps which should be taken to reach the desired end. So I account it worth while to put before you what seem to me some of the necessary conditions of the Reform of ourselves and our system on Christian lines. There will be nothing original or startling in what I have to say; but it will be for you to consider and judge whether thoughts, which are no doubt familiar to you all in some form, are wise and practicable as I express them; whether, in fact, this is the way or one way of persuading mankind to give a fair trial to Christianity as a general rule of life and conduct.

And first, as is perhaps natural to one of my education and calling, I place the *Importance of having*

[1] 1 John ii. 2.　　　[2] 1 Tim. ii. 3, 4.

a Christian Clergy. The phrase sounds perhaps paradoxical, even flippant. I may seem to you to have slipped into a fault of taste while straining after an epigram. Nothing is further from my intention than to speak lightly on so serious a topic. And on the other hand, while I use the words in all sad earnest, I have no wish to set up as a censor of better men than myself. But I do see that there are special difficulties in the way of clergymen at the present day being really Christian, and those difficulties are not always surmounted. If the idea that it is hard for a clergyman to be a Christian is strange to any of you, let me speak for a moment of those special difficulties. I need not dwell long on what I feel most, the temptations which beset an academic clergyman, college tutor or schoolmaster, the greater part of whose work necessarily lies in secular study and routine of business; temptations to coldness and unspirituality; for those temptations are obvious. But it does not seem to me to be really any easier for parish priests, whose life is more ostensibly occupied with sacred things. I have no doubt that in the last fifty years the clergy have improved greatly in energy and system, and in devotion to the Church as a divinely ordained society. But in those very virtues are their corresponding dangers. No doubt parish work in the old days was too often slipshod and ineffective; but it is possible to give too much value to the externals of organization, and so fall into idolatry. A clergyman is tempted to be content if the machinery of his parish is running smoothly, if the clubs and societies are full and active, the services bright and well attended. He may spend himself utterly on these things; and yet be starving the souls of his people and his own soul; growing hard and unspiritual and self-satisfied. Then enthusiasm for the Church is not always tempered by charity; it makes men judge those that are without, and not always judge them fairly.

But after all, system and energy and enthusiasm are good things in themselves, and need only to be touched by the sweet reasonableness of the Spirit of Christ to make them good in the using. But there are failings for which so much cannot be said. Perhaps the greatest cause which makes us unprofitable servants to-day is Ignorance. The English Clergy was once called the Wonder of the World for its learning; but compared with the lay folk it is a learned clergy no longer. It is, of course, nothing but good that the general standard has risen; and it would be absurd to expect a busy parish priest to keep abreast of the latest word that has been written either on Theology, or on social questions. But there are two things every clergyman must know, if he is to be a minister of Christ—his Bible and his people.

As a Church we must use intelligent criticism and sincere exegesis if we are to understand what is the Word of God, and be listened to by educated people. As individuals we need, perhaps more, that deep and exact knowledge of the Sacred Text, which I think is very rare among candidates for Orders, but is worth more than all other learning for purposes of teaching and devotion. There is so much to read, so much to learn nowadays, that it is hard to get such a knowledge of the Bible. Yet we must get it; and we must get a knowledge of our people, and learn what are the wants and perplexities of the present day, before we can minister to them. And that is hard too. Prejudice stands in the way, and the inertia which it is truer to call weariness than sloth. Some of us are too busy, and some of us, I fear, are too much bound by convention and custom, and a sense of what is due to our position, to enter fully and sincerely into the thoughts and needs of our lay brethren. And the problem of feeling and winning sympathy is certainly not made easier for clergymen by the fact that they are ministers of a State Church. The cares of this World and the deceitfulness of riches are ever present with us in a somewhat acute form. I am unwilling to embark in a digression upon the advantages and disadvantages of Establishment; but it is a subject which in this connection cannot be passed over without a word; because the question of Disestablishment does not lie in the remote or near future, but is present with us and urgent. Against the separation of Church and State, there is a large body of honest sentiment, and a perfectly reasonable desire to retain what is admitted to be only an ideal, until it can be again fulfilled in fact; and there is the fear of dislocation and confusion, and the check to spiritual work, especially in country districts, which that separation would entail before the

Church was able to reorganize its system and its Ministry on an independent basis. On the other side, it is pleaded that a Privy Council and a House of Commons, which rightly contain men of any religious belief and no religious belief, are impossible as a final Court of Appeal in questions of Discipline, and much more so in questions of Doctrine; that a supposed State endowment encourages the laity in an entirely false view of their duty in maintaining their Church; and finally, that in the matter of privilege the Church of England is virtually disestablished already, and that the remnants of privilege are dearly bought at the price of liberty. Churchmen begin to question whether it is not worth while to recognize publicly the fact that the Church of England is no longer a National Church, as a first step to making it one, if possible. It should, moreover, be remembered that the cry for Disestablishment comes no longer only from the opponents of the Church. For one clergyman who held such views thirty years ago, there must be ten to-day who wish for Disestablishment, and a hundred who view the prospect of it calmly and dispassionately. The question is no longer whether the Church can escape Disestablishment, but whether it can tolerate Establishment in the present conditions.

However, I do not wish to press the view that an Established Church is really a fatal hindrance to the Christianity of its Clergy, for I do not believe it. There is a far more serious difficulty in the way of all who are set apart, in whatever religious body, for

the Ministry of the Word and Sacraments—a personal
and moral difficulty. On the one hand, we all feel
that it is indispensable to an effective Ministry that
the life of the Minister should be as near to the
principles of the Religion which he teaches, as by
God's Grace he can make it. On the other hand, it
is inevitable, if we are to be guides and prophets at
all, that we should preach better than we live; because
Religion is a greater and a holier thing than the life
of the best of men. We have this treasure in earthen
vessels. And this necessity involves a double danger.
There is a real danger that a man who is occupied
in studying and teaching the Life of Christ, when he
looks on it and on the weakness and imperfection of
his own life, may be cast down and discouraged by
the terrible contrast, and so be tempted to relax his
efforts both in teaching and living. And if this seems
to you a fanciful and morbid apprehension, there is
at least no doubt about that other instant danger,
that one who has perhaps attained some success as a
preacher or a counsellor may be content with that;
and, even while he is still thinking to guide others
in the Way, grow cold in his own Religion, careless
in his own life. The fear that haunted St. Paul is
still for every ordained Minister not a terror only,
but a danger: μή πως ἄλλοις κηρύξας αὐτὸς ἀδόκιμος
γένωμαι.[1]

My brethren, pray for us. And pray also for
yourselves, for under God you are responsible for us;

[1] 1 Cor. ix. 27.

and that not only because it is from the ranks of the
laity that the Clergy are called, and the Christian
home does more in the moulding of the true Priest
than any other human agency; not only because in
your hands it lies to keep us true to our vows and
to exact from us the best we have to give in Life
and Doctrine; but because in very truth you share
with us this Priesthood. I am a firm believer in the
Sacrament of Holy Orders. I deliberately call it a
Sacrament as being neither a magical ceremony, nor
merely a decent form with no particular meaning.
I would not abate or change one word of our Ordination
service, for I hold that God has given the Church
authority to delegate to the Priest and the Bishop
spiritual functions which no man can rightly discharge
unless he be duly ordained thereto. But neither are
the duly ordained ministers to discharge them as being
lords over God's heritage, but as servants of all—
servants of men as well as of God. Indeed, they
cannot discharge them otherwise in any true sense.
The people are every whit as necessary to corporate
worship as the Minister, and that not merely as represented
by him, or as listeners and lookers-on. Without
their active co-operation the office and authority of the
priesthood is a thing meaningless and profane, inconsistent
not only with the idea of a Church, but with
the idea of Christianity. We have reason to be
thankful that the Church of England has so plainly
marked her sense of this truth in the Book of Common
Prayer. It has been pointed out to us lately that

the Daily Offices cannot properly be said except with a congregation; the moral of which is, I take it, not that the Clergy should give up daily services, but that people should go to them. And in the Great Service of all, the priesthood of the laity is emphasized with no uncertain sound. The Rite of Holy Communion not only may not, but cannot, be celebrated without people as well as Minister.

And if you as laity have a right to your part in the Ministry of Worship, with its corresponding obligation, you have a still more undoubted part in the Ministry of Conversion, the Apostolic office of evangelizing the World. I do not mean that every Christian man and woman is bound forthwith to go to the ends of the earth or to the East End of London, and be a missionary in the technical sense. I do not suggest that it is everybody's duty, or the duty of more than a very few in each generation, to give up their lives to definite social and religious work. For many people, to do so would be a desertion of duty; it might even be self-indulgence masquerading as heroism. The daily work of the world has to be kept going; and the great majority of men and women are bound, first, to earn their own living, and then to serve those few whom God has put close to them in this world; "to make upon the whole a family happier by their presence." It is by this, by minding our own business in a true and noble sense, that most of us are called on to do our evangelizing. This is a homely and disappointing doctrine for ardent souls;

and I am half ashamed to enforce it by so trite a saying.   But it cannot be repeated too often that a Christian Life is the best argument for the Truth of Christianity as a Creed.   It is the only argument that unconverted Humanity will attend to; and I think unconverted Humanity is right.   But further, it is clear that a Christian life, lived in normal circumstances, is more impressive and encouraging than one lived in special conditions; so that the genuine layman has an advantage as a missionary over the clergyman and the philanthropist.   To *be* a Christian in any genuine sense is to preach the Gospel, and that perhaps in the hardest and most efficient way.   But the apostolate of the laity may find, and if the spirit is there inevitably does find, directer methods.   The right attitude of mind towards our fellow-creatures brings or discovers opportunities of service; and service gives the unresented claim to speak a word in season.

There is, moreover, another reason, deeper and more intimate even than the right to share in worship and evangelization, why a Christian Laity is not only desirable but necessary in order to the fulfilment of the purpose of the Incarnation and the existence of a Christian Church.   And that reason lies in the Christian verity of which I have spoken before, the equal value of every soul before God—equal value and equal responsibility.

Plato[1] has taught us that a State or a Society as a whole may claim certain qualities in right of

Republic, iv. 428, 429.

their existence in a portion of itself. Thus a State may be called wise if its government is wise; and brave, if its soldiers are brave. But when it comes to the continent Virtue, δικαιοσύνη, Righteousness, it must be everywhere or nowhere. Not only is it desirable that every citizen should possess and manifest that virtue, but it is not possible for it to exist without the co-operation of all classes and individuals; for it is essentially a *relation* of class to class, and man to man, and of the whole Society to the Divine Principle, Immanent and Transcendent. What Plato called δικαιοσύνη, we, to whom Christ has been made known, call Christianity : the *knowledge* of our right relation to God and our fellow-men, and a *life* of thought and action in harmony with that relation. But this life cannot be fully lived, this knowledge cannot be fully attained, except by common action based upon a lively sense of individual responsibility to the whole and for the whole. A society cannot properly be called religious because a part of it is religious. A Christian Clergy is a true and fruitful element in a Christian Church, but it does not in itself constitute a Christian Church, much less a Christian Nation. The true purpose and Constitution of a Christian Society is set forth in very different terms by St. Paul in the Epistle to the Ephesians : "That we . . . may grow up in all things unto Him which is the head, even Christ ; from whom all the body fitly framed and knit together, through that which every joint supplieth, according to the working in due measure of each several part, maketh the increase of the body unto the building up of itself in love." [1]

I have laid stress upon this thought, because I seem to detect in the laity, while they are quick to resent clerical dictation or encroachment, a tendency to let the clergy perform for them at least a part of their duty ; to make them their Vicars, as the great Monasteries did with poor priests in the Middle Ages, for the discharge of certain of their religious functions. But it is not safe to neglect one part of what claims the whole life, if it is a reality at all. To omit the outward realization of the Communion of Saints is to weaken its influence upon thought and action. People who are content to go to church by deputy may well be tempted to think they can depute other activities of the Christian life as well. *Facilis descensus.* And if the clergy cannot rightly offer public worship to God on your behalf without you, much less can any ministry of theirs take the place of your private prayer and conscious communion with God, which is the spring and the renewal of spiritual life. No one and nothing can take the place of that. It is possible to be too busy even with well-doing to do it really well ; to be anxious and troubled about many things, and yet to miss the one thing needful, the gracious presence of the Master. And that no man can win and keep for us. "No man may deliver his brother, nor make agreement to God for him." We shall not be asked in that Day whether we have been priests or laymen—

[1] Eph. iv. 15, 16.

for there will not be a different rule and measure for one and the other—but whether we have tried to mould our lives as disciples of Christ, and the true brethren of all men. There will be a very stringent test of orthodoxy for those who are to be saved; even the ὀρθὴ δόξα, child and parent of courage and humility, which dares to see Him as He is, and so to grow like Him. The proof of right belief will be right action. The sentence of acceptance or rejection is, " Inasmuch as ye did it—or did it not—unto one of the least of these My brethren." Yet we must remember that the act of charity is the outward, visible sign of a Sacrament; the cup of cold water does not lose its reward, for that it is given " in a Name because ye are Christ's."

I have spoken of the Judgment as future; but it is as true, and perhaps more profitable, to think of it as passing upon our lives daily and hourly in the present. We *are* asked now if we are doing our best to make the world Christian by being Christians ourselves in the wide and not in the narrow sense.

3. Since I began to deliver these Lectures, more than one person has asked me, " But what remedy do you propose for the conditions you describe?" I have been quite rightly told that I raise more questions than I solve. That is, of course, inevitable in dealing with such a subject as I have chosen, especially when the preacher has no better equipment of knowledge and character than I can claim. But it was also my deliberate

purpose to raise more questions than I can answer, in the hope of getting some of them answered by wiser and better people than myself; and in the hope of raising doubts whether we are going the right way in our attempts to answer others. I desire to make people, especially people in Oxford, discontented, to make them think and wonder and inquire whether all is well, and if all is not well, how it is to be mended; and I shall have succeeded so far, if my words help, even in a small degree, in bringing the fine intellect and character of Oxford to give itself to the solution of the riddles which perplex and threaten us. But on the other hand, I wish publicly to record my conviction that the most and the hardest of these problems cannot be solved at all—*directly*; that the methods we are tempted to use with them are, as I have said, methods which treat symptoms, and leave the root of the mischief untouched. Whenever we try to cure a particular social evil by dead lift, by legislation merely, or the expenditure of money, we commonly find that we create a new trouble and perhaps a worse; we are beset by two hydra-heads for one. For instance, it is idle to rail at economic laws, it is ruinous to disregard or transgress them; because, so long as men are governed by the principle of selfishness, economic laws are the correct formula for recording and foretelling their mutual relations. There is no lasting escape from them, either in blinding ourselves to their cogency, or in artificially exempting limited areas from their operation. But Christian thought has learned to look upon Miracles as the manifestation of the Divine Will transcending natural laws for a moral purpose. And I believe the Miracle which can alone deliver us from the inexorable tyranny of economic laws is the influence of Christ upon Human character.

I fear that in saying this I may disappoint some of my hearers. I must at least renounce all claim to be a prophet for those who look for a speedy and dramatic solution of our difficulties; a millennium dating from to-morrow or next year. To such, the Reformation I propose will appear tedious and common-place. And so, in a sense, it is, inasmuch as I have no novel or startling message. The Gospel I am trying to preach is near nineteen centuries old; the way to its fulfilment is long and laborious, and we have almost forgotten that it is heroic. Though men should embrace it to-day, neither we who are met here, nor our sons, nor our grandsons, would see its full realization; yet I know that its acceptance would be the first step, the step that counts, in the redemption of the World from moral evil, and gradually from much of physical and material evil as well. If all the men and women who call themselves Christians could simply do the good they know, and eschew the evil they know, for Christ's sake, the aspect of social and economic problems would be so changed that we have no right to suppose that they would remain insoluble. And the way, I believe the only way, to that change is the training of Christian character in the individual, and

o

the formation of Christian public opinion, sure of itself and not afraid to speak.

4. Christian public opinion, the expression of the Spirit of Christ in the united will, emotion, and intellect of human societies, has wrought, and is working, miracles.   It has raised the standard of purity, of honesty, of loving-kindness ; and above all, and including all, it has established the sense of brotherhood, of mutual obligation and responsibility.   But it has not had its perfect work.   It has been paralyzed by timidity, the fear of persecution and ridicule, the fear of plain speaking ; it has been seduced by temptation, the personal desire for ease and pleasure, the corporate desire for power and wealth.   But more than all, it has been weakened by division, and obscured by controversy and by an exaggerated sense of the paramount duty of withstanding erring brethren to the face because they are to be blamed.   The greatest and most deadly effect of controversy is not that it embitters, but that it confuses.   While Christianity seemed to hold the field, Christians have sometimes, in all sincerity, been so much occupied with minor differences that they have forgotten the real issue.   But surely for us to-day, unless we wilfully blind ourselves to the signs of the times, that issue is clear and definite.   The alternative has always been, but now it is very plainly between Christian and non-Christian.

On one side stands the World, the principle of Selfishness.   But here we must be on our guard against labelling people, or sets of people, who do not agree

with us " the World," and treating them as enemies.
That may be Old Testament Religion, but it is not
Gospel. " We wrestle not against flesh and blood, but
against principalities, against powers, against the rulers
of the darkness of this world, against spiritual wickedness in high places." [1]

On one side stands the World, and on the other
the Disciples—that is, all who in *Belief* accept the
Incarnation and what it implies, and in *Practice* take
Christ's teaching as their rule. His life as their pattern,
and Himself as their motive and their strength. The
belief and the practice are inseparable; the Life is
the only test and guarantee of the soundness of the
Creed.

We cannot ask more than that of the brethren; and
we may not ask less, if we believe that in Him alone
we have life, and that His coming was the beginning of
the full and final revelation.

Now if we accept *ex animo* this definition of
Christianity, it must make a notable change in our
relation to Christians of other denominations; and
it will bring home to us with new force the saying
of our Lord, "He that is not against us is on our part."
These words are commonly interpreted in practice to
mean that we may join with Roman Catholics and
Protestant Nonconformists in social and moral work;
but they must mean more than that: we must join
with them also in the definitely Religious work of
maintaining the essential unity of the Christian Creed

[1] Eph. vi. 12.

and Life; that is, if we wish Christianity in any form to rule the World.

The common objection to such union of Religious work by differing sects is that it involves a sacrifice of Principle. That objection I would try to answer in two ways. First, with the history of Christian disunion before us, we are bound to examine ourselves stringently as to what we mean by "Principle," and inquire whether we are called on to give up certain things we value highly for the sake of the strength of Unity; and I think we ought to be prepared to go some way for that end. But second, we are not called upon to give up anything which is really "Principle," anything that is truly a means of Grace for us. An external and mechanical uniformity in worship and in the minor details of belief is now, humanly speaking, impossible; and we are beginning to question if it be desirable or necessary. If we once admit that a man can be truly a Christian in any Church or sect but our own, we have surrendered the whole position; and surely we all admit that. Every man is permitted and bound to adopt the symbols in which Eternal Truth comes with life and power to his own soul. Christ comes to the Roman Catholic in Confession and the Mass; He comes to the Presbyterian in the bare-walled kirk, the unfettered prayer, the infrequent and solemn Communion; to us He comes in the stately, reasonable services of our Church, with their appeal neglecting, as it seems to us, neither the senses nor the intellect. And if He comes to all,

all are one, for He is one. And none may despise his fellow or his fellow's religion ; for " No man can say that Jesus is the Lord but through the Holy Ghost."

The union of the sanctified life goes beyond forms of ecclesiastical government ; it is something higher and deeper than the questions of doctrine and worship which divide us. If we are really trying to live the Christian life, to be true followers of Him who, when He was reviled, reviled not again, when He suffered, threatened not, then we are in the truest and deepest sense promoting the unity of the Church of Christ, and claiming brotherhood with all those who are doing the like in all parts of Christendom.

It is to these, the real Christians in every Church and sect and denomination, that God has committed the task of bringing mankind back to Him. Such a body of Christians exists, as we testify Sunday by Sunday, when we speak in the Bidding Prayer of " Christ's holy Catholic Church, that is, the whole congregation of Christian people dispersed throughout the whole World." But they are estranged and divided, they are suspicious and discouraged. If only they could come to know and understand one another—to forget their differences, and remember only that they are one in Christ Jesus !

I understand that it has been said of me that I draw too dark a picture of the conditions of life in Christian lands. I fear it is not so, but I know too that there is another side to the picture. Christianity is not a Failure, except when we compare it with what it might have been, what yet shall be. For as it has been the salt of the world, so it is the hope of the world ; and the Spirit of Love is even now working towards its perfect consummation. If I did not believe that, I should lose faith in God and man. And without faith, I should not have had the patience or the effrontery to write and deliver these Lectures.

Let me end, then, by trying to set before you my vision of the days that are coming—a vision which, I trust, is not altogether fancy. I see the rise of a new Religious Order, the greatest that the World has known, drawn from all nations and all classes, and, what seems stranger yet, from all Churches. Its members bear no distinctive habit; no distinctive name, if it be not the humble name of Disciples. Yet they are known to each other, and their knowledge is strength, for they are all the men and women who are not afraid to confess Christ both with their lips and in their lives. Their Rule is brief and simple ; it has but two clauses, " Bear ye one another's burdens, and so fulfil the Law of Christ." Their common Creed is a belief in the Person of Christ and in His power to make men like Him. In their common worship they are united in spirit, though not, it may be, in place and ritual. Each is loyal to the Church which brings his soul nearest to God ; yet does not judge his brother who finds another way the best. For they have learned that God, who is one, fulfils Himself in many ways, and that the bond that joins them is stronger than the outward symbols which divide them.

And, as I look, it seems to me that their brotherhood has changed the aspect of the World. The outward change is notable here and there. Monstrous wealth is gone, with its apparatus of luxury and ostentation; and miserable poverty and degradation are gone, with their apparatus of tavern and jail and workhouse. But Mankind still go about their business and their pleasure; there is still toil and rest, still joy and sorrow, still success and failure. Yet there *is* rest and reward for the toiler; the mourner is comforted; there is no arrogance in success, no bitterness in failure; because Christians have learned, and mankind is learning, that the cause of every man is the cause of all men, and the Cause of God.

THE END

PRINTED BY
WILLIAM CLOWES AND SONS, LIMITED,
LONDON AND BECCLES.